Learn to Play Recorders in Harmony

English & Español Level One: Empathy Songs

Sarah Samuelson
STUDIO

www.sarahsamuelsonstudio.com

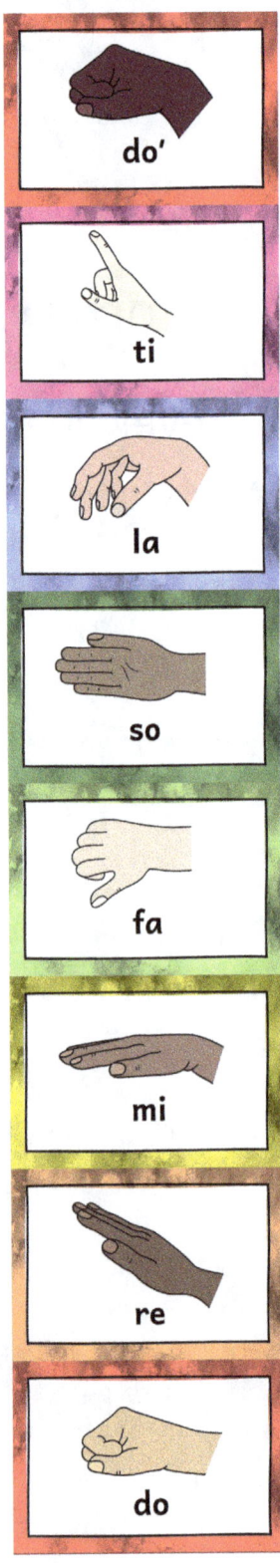

Copyright © 2024 Sarah Samuelson Studio
All Rights Reserved.

No part of this publication may be reproduced or transmitted in any form
without permission from the publisher.

Learn to Play Recorders in Harmony Level One Contents

do, G
1. Introduction to Rhythm — 1
2. We are Part of this Beautiful World — 5
   Español - Formamos Parte de este Hermoso Mundo — 7

do-re, G-A
3. I Have Worth — 8
   Español - Creo que tengo valor — 10
4. I Can Show Empathy — 11
   Español - Puedo mostrar empatía — 13

do-re-mi, G-A-B
5. Do-Re-Mi Body Tap — 14
   Words Can Be Healing to Say — 15
   Español - Las palabras tienen poder curativo — 16
6. Welcome Here   harmony: round — 17
   Español - Bienvenido aqui (England: Hot Cross Buns) & Hot Cross Buns — 19
7. I Can Be a Friend — 21
   Español - Puedo ser un amigo (France: Au Clair de la Lune) — 22
8. Leap for Joy — 23
   Español - Salta de Alegría (Hop Old Squirrel) — 25
9. I Can Be More Understanding — 26
   Español - Puedo ser más comprensivo (Spiritual: Babylon's Falling) — 28

do-re-mi-so, G-A-B-D
10. Put Yourself in Their Shoes — 29
    Español - Ponte en su Lugar (Spiritual: Oh, I'm Goin' to Sing) — 31
11. We Want All to Feel Connected — 32
    Español - Queremos ke todos se sientan conectados (USA: Mary Had a Little Lamb) — 34
12. We Each Have a Family — 35
    Español - Cado uno tiene una familia (USA: Johnny Works with One Hammer) — 37
13. Little Changes Make a Difference — 38
    Español - Pequeños cambios marcan la diferencia (Robert Lowry) — 40

do-re-mi-fa-so, G-A-B-C-D
14. Our Voice is Important — 42
    Español - Nuestra voz importa (Bohemian Folk Song) — 44
15. Stay Hopeful — 45
    Español - Puedo tener esperanza — 47

LOW so-la-do-re-mi-so, D-E-G-A-B-C-D
16. Care for My Neighbor — 48
    Español - Cuidar a mi Vecino (Germany: Mäh, Lämmchen, Mäh) — 50
17. We Want Justice in Our World — 51
    Español - Queremos Justicia en Nuestro Mundo (Spiritual: Oh!Oh! Freedom) — 53

NEW KEY of D: do-re-mi-fa-so, D-E-F#-G-A
18. You are Important — 54
    Español - Eres importante (England: Here Comes a Bluebird) — 57

KEY of D: do-re-mi-fa-so-la, D-E-F#-G-A-B
19. We Can Learn to Express Our Emotions — 58
    Español - Aprendemos a expresar emociones (Argentina: Los elefantes) — 60
20. We are Like Stars in the Night — 61
    Español - Somos como estrella en la Noche (France: Twinkle, Twinkle) — 63
    English - Twinkle, Twinkle, Little Star — 64
    Español - Spanish Estrellita Donde Estas — 65
    Français - Ah! Vous dirai-je, Maman — 66
21. We all Have a Super Power — 67
    Español - Todos tenemos un superpoder (Mexico: Chocolate molinillo) — 69
22. I am Learning to Regulate   harmony: round — 70
    Español - Estoy aprendiendo a regularme (Japan: Kaeru No Uta) — 72
    Japanese - Kaeru No Uta — 73
    Chords & Intervals - Level 1 — 75

Copyright©2024 by Sarah Samuelson Studio. All rights reserved. Printed in the USA.

Learn to Play in Harmony Recorder Level 1

Learn to Play in Harmony is a curriculum for learning how to read music by singing and playing the recorders. The solfège method assigns each note in the music scale with a syllable: do-re-mi-fa-so-la-ti-do as heard in the song "doe a deer...ray a drop of golden sun...me a name I call myself." This curriculum starts with songs only using do, then do-re, then do-re-mi and so on. Melodies are songs from different countries and African American spirituals. Here are the steps for learning. Many people will skip the solfège and go right to the note names. My experience has been that those who learn with solfège and note names will build a tonal memory that over time will help you learn songs more quickly.

The Sing and Play Process of Learning

Learn the solfège
1) Practice the hand signs – it helps you remember the solfège
2) Practice the fingerings while singing the solfège - it helps your fingers get used to feeling the recorder wholes and hearing the melody and the solfège will help you remember the relationship between the pitches (steps or skips or repeated notes)
3) Play the note and think the solfège as you play

Learn the note names
4) Practice the fingerings while singing the note names – B-A-G - Taking time to do both of these steps will help you build your tonal memory stronger.
5) Play the notes and think the note names as you play

Learn the lyrics
6) Sing the lyrics in the language you are most familiar with then sing in the language your friends are most familiar with. This is a great way learn about empathy!
7) Practice the fingerings while saying the lyrics.
8) Play the note and think the lyrics as you play.

Bring your own creativity
9) Once you've learned the song start improvising or creating your own version! Remember the rhythms are only simplified for learning.
    a) Change the rhythms
    b) Think of new lyrics.

Continue to learn more melodies and harmony
10) Reinforce empathy
11) Continue learning solfège, music theory and languages and lots of rounds to sing in choir or with small ensembles in Level 2, 3, 4 and more. If you have any questions contact info@sarahsamuelsonstudio.com. Happy singing!

Copyright©2024 by Sarah Samuelson Studio
All rights reserved. Printed in the USA.

Lesson 1: Rhythm - Walk, Jog & Rest

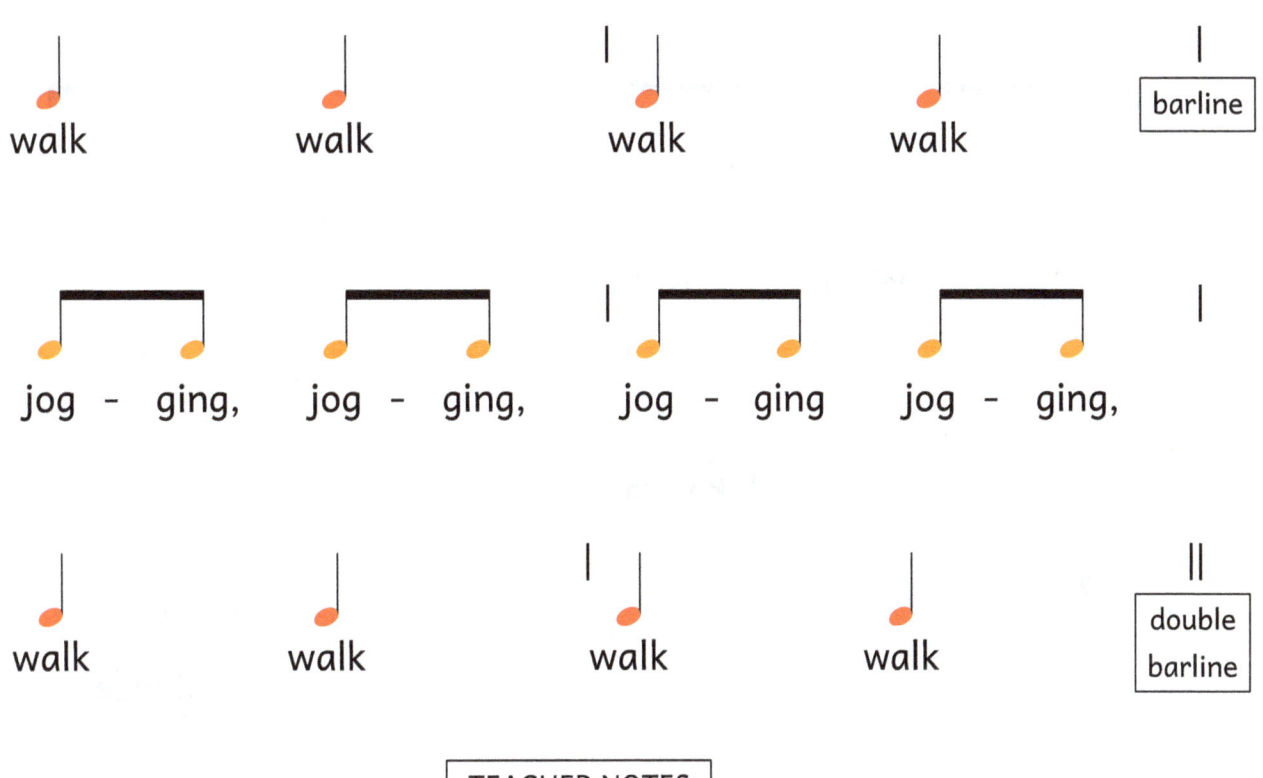

TEACHER NOTES

Speak the words in a steady beat to get to know the timing of the notes.
Speak the words as you walk and jog and keep a steady beat.

Copyright © 2024 Sarah Samuelson Studio

Rhythm in Speech

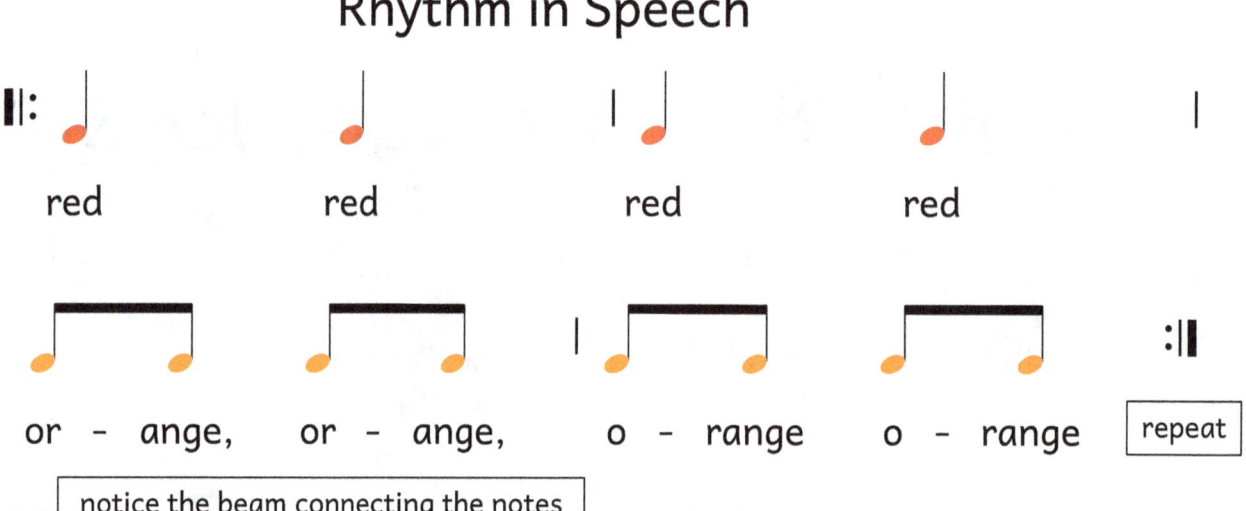

Rhythm in Silence

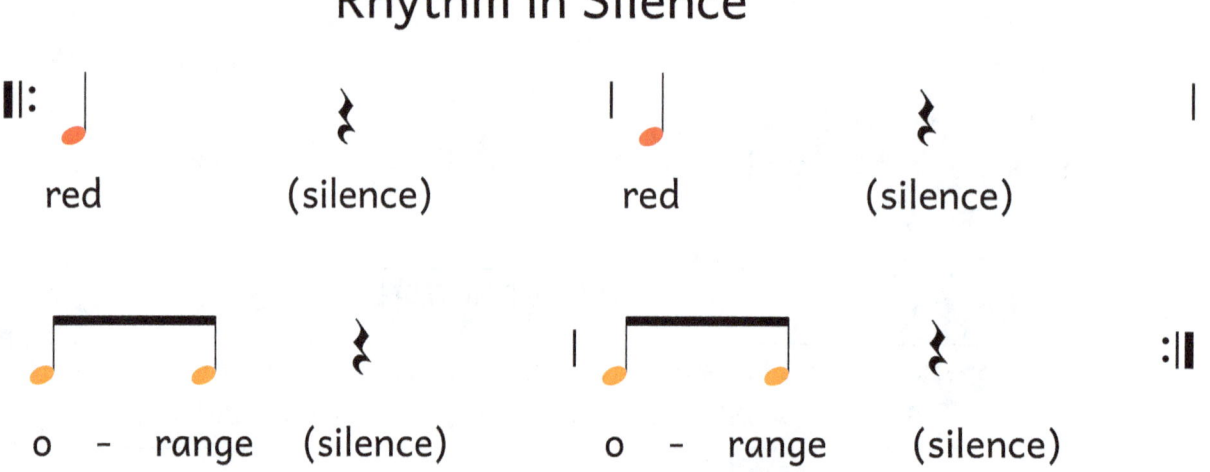

Copyright © 2024 Sarah Samuelson Studio

Quarter Notes

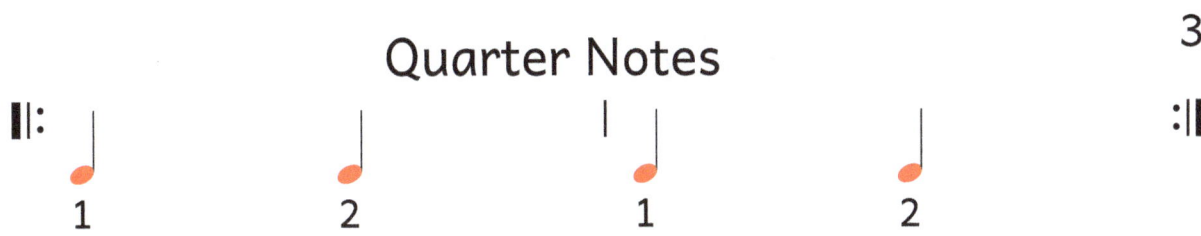

When counting quarter and eighth notes it is best to "subdivide" which means to add the "and" when counting the quarter notes so that your eighth notes can be more even.

Eighth Notes

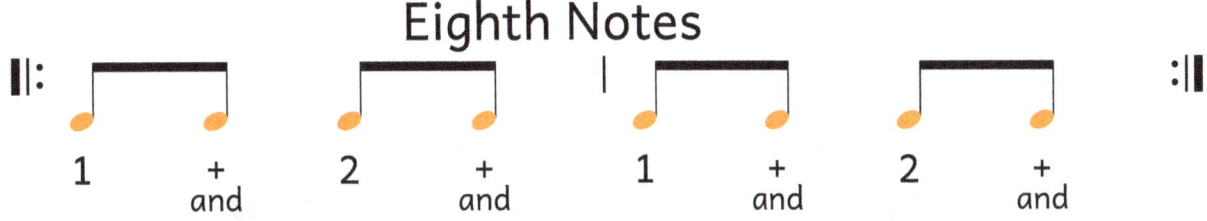

Quarter Notes & Rests

Eighth Notes & Rests

Quarter Notes & Eighth Notes & Rests

Copyright © 2024 Sarah Samuelson Studio

Solfège G Major Scale

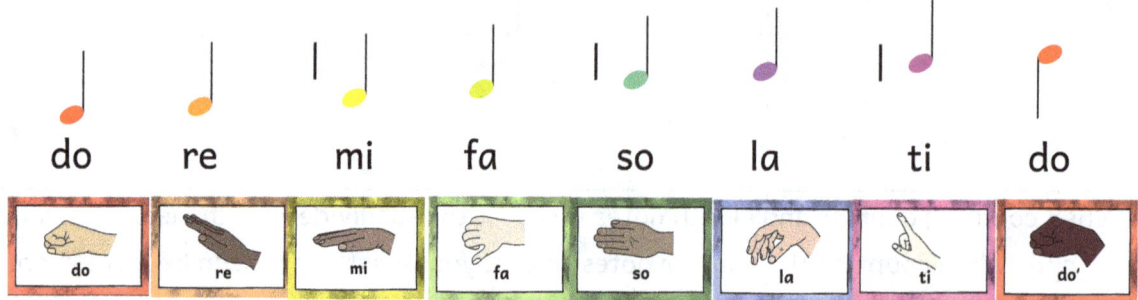

Solfège G Major Scale for Piano

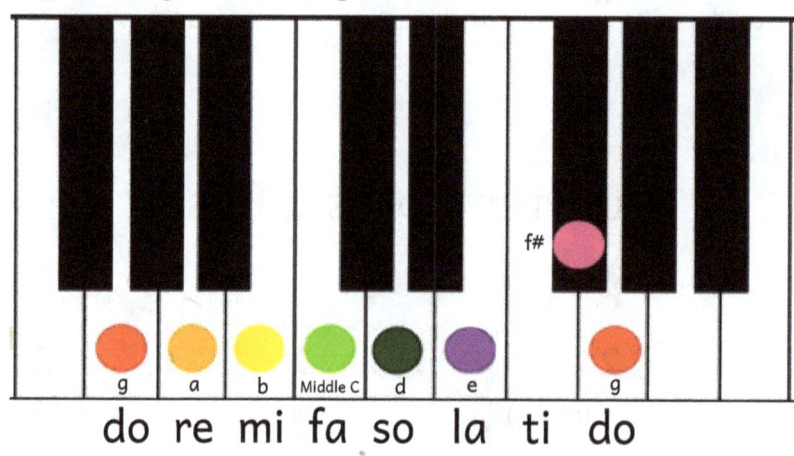

Chords for Piano

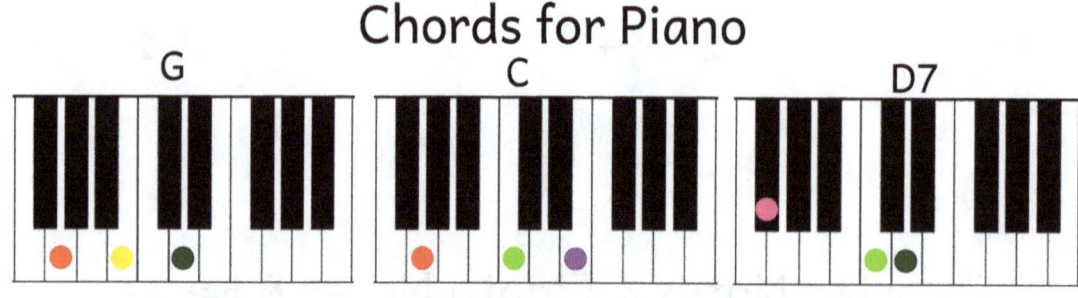

Copyright © 2024 Sarah Samuelson Studio

Lesson 2: do, G
We are Part of this Beautiful World
Music: Sarah Samuelson

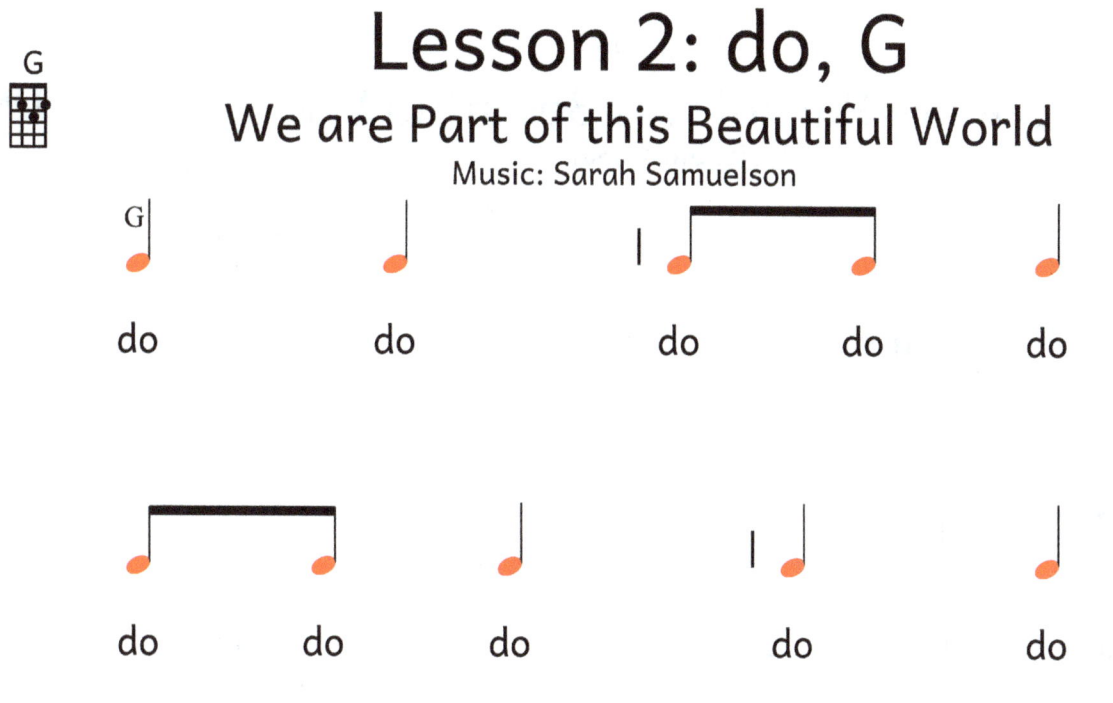

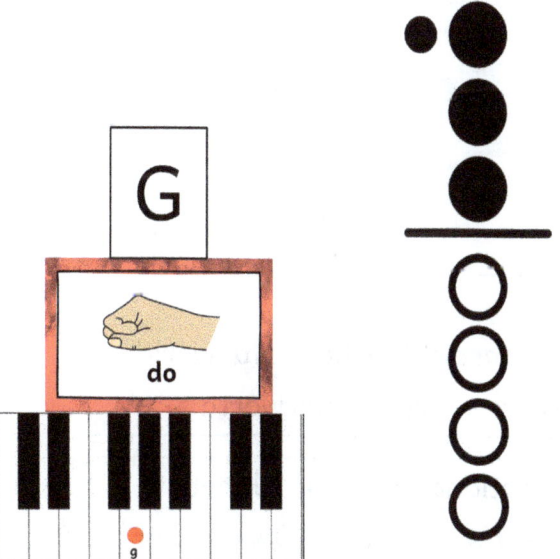

Copyright © 2024 Sarah Samuelson Studio

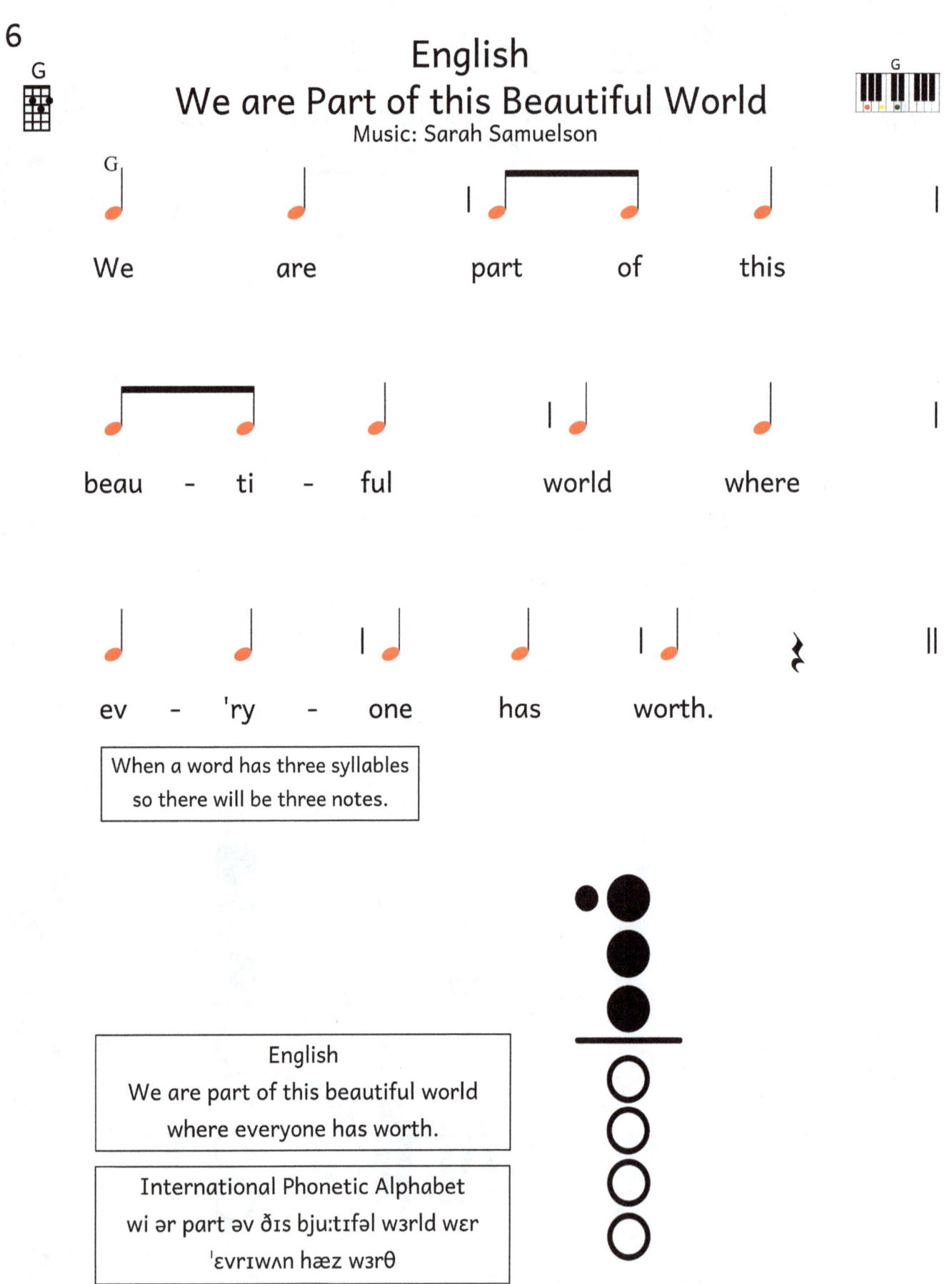

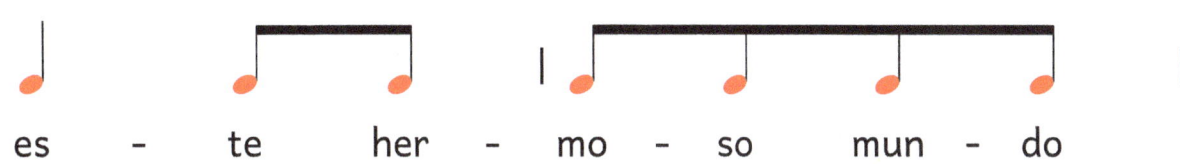

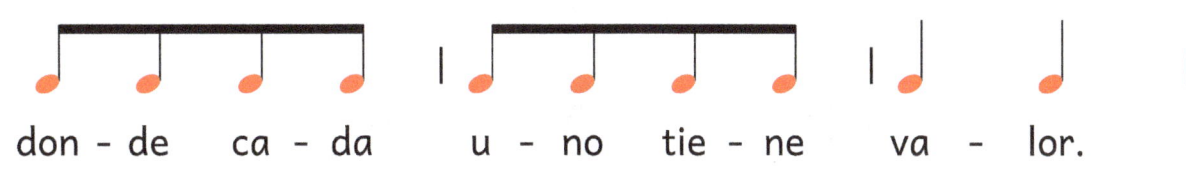

Español
Formamos parte de este hermoso mundo
donde cada uno tiene valor.

International Phonetic Alphabet
ˈfɔrmamos ˈparte ðe ˈeste erˈmoso ˈmundo
ˈdonde ˈkada ˈuno ˈtiene ˈba.lor.

Copyright © 2024 Sarah Samuelson Studio

Lesson 3: do-re
I Have Worth
Music: Sarah Samuelson

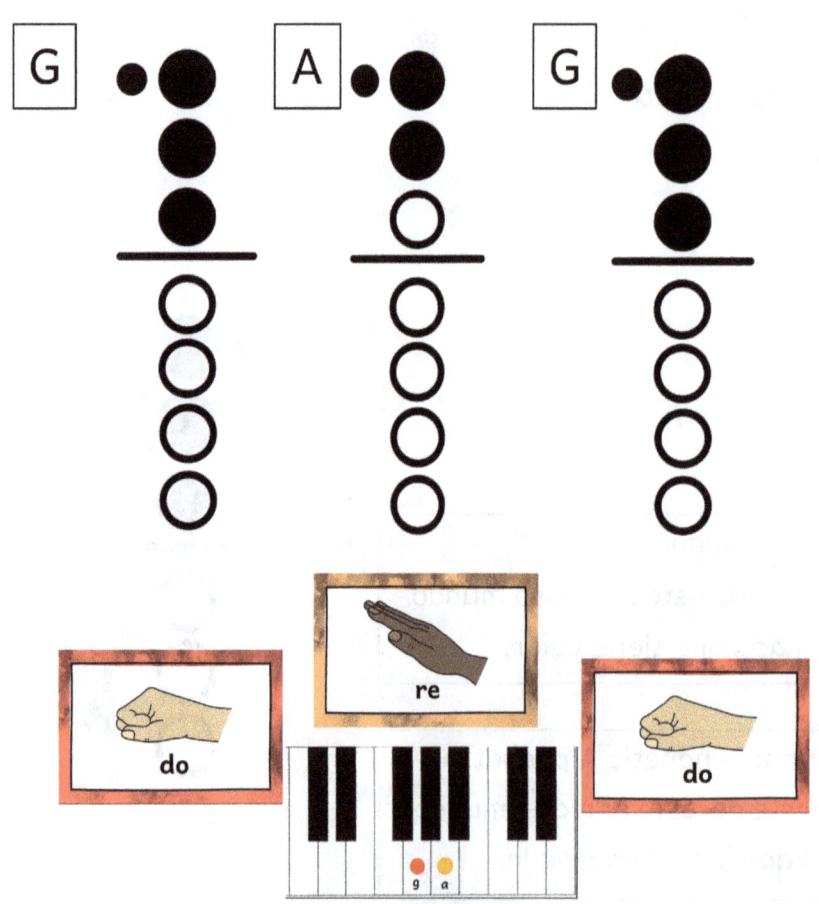

Copyright © 2024 Sarah Samuelson Studio

English
I Have Worth
Music: Sarah Samuelson

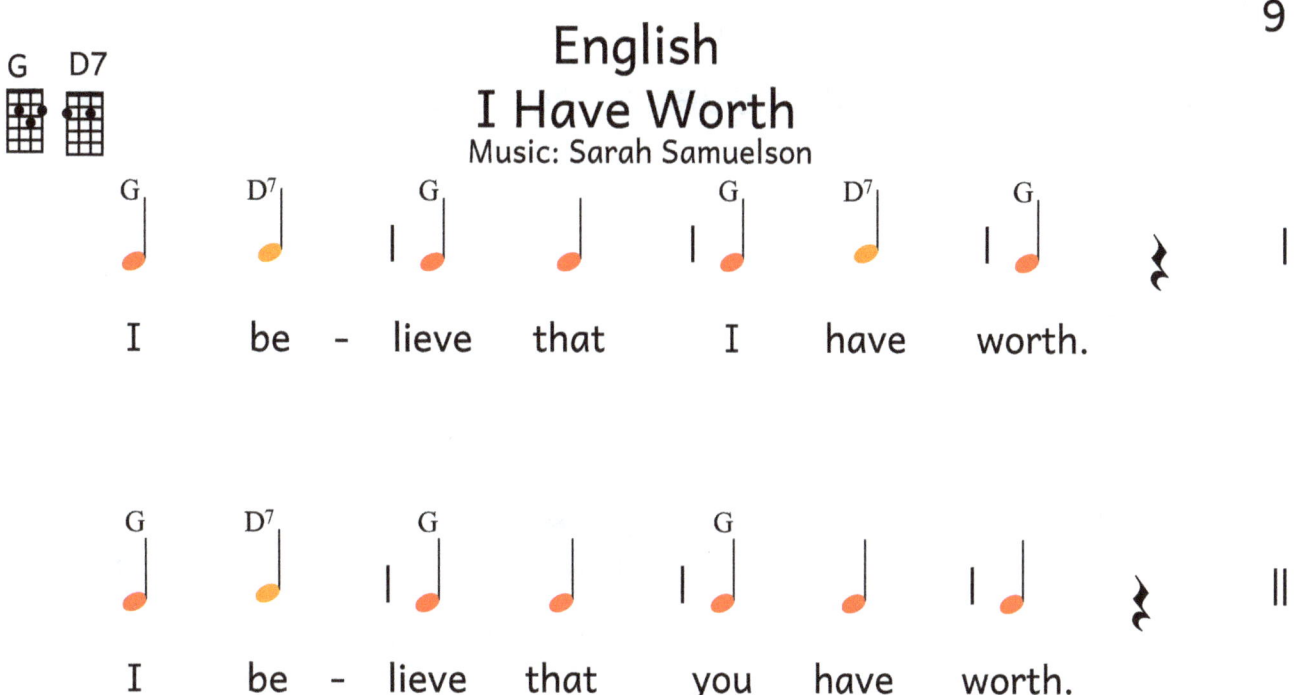

I be - lieve that I have worth.

I be - lieve that you have worth.

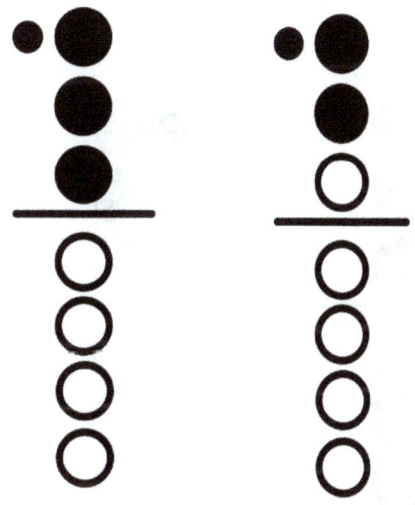

International Phonetic Alphabet	Actions
aɪ bɪˈliːv ðæt aɪ hæv wɜːrθ aɪ bɪˈliːv ðæt juː hæv wɜːrθ	Walk around the classroom as you sing this song and point to others when singing, "You have worth."

Copyright © 2024 Sarah Samuelson Studio

Español
Creo que tengo valor
Music: Sarah Samuelson

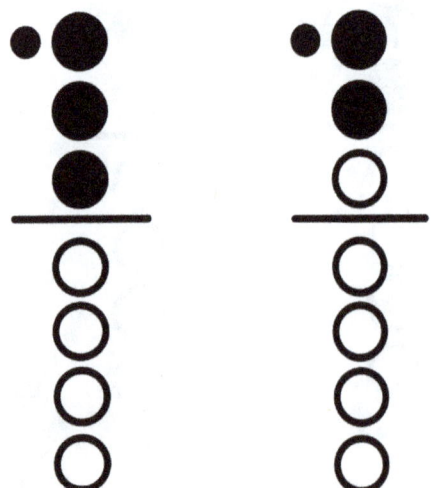

Español	International Phonetic Alphabet
Creo que tengo valor	kreo ke ˈtengo βaˈlor.
Creo que tienes valor	ˈkreo ke ˈtjenes βaˈlor.

Lesson 4: do-re-do, G-A
I Can Show Empathy
Text & Music: Sarah Samuelson

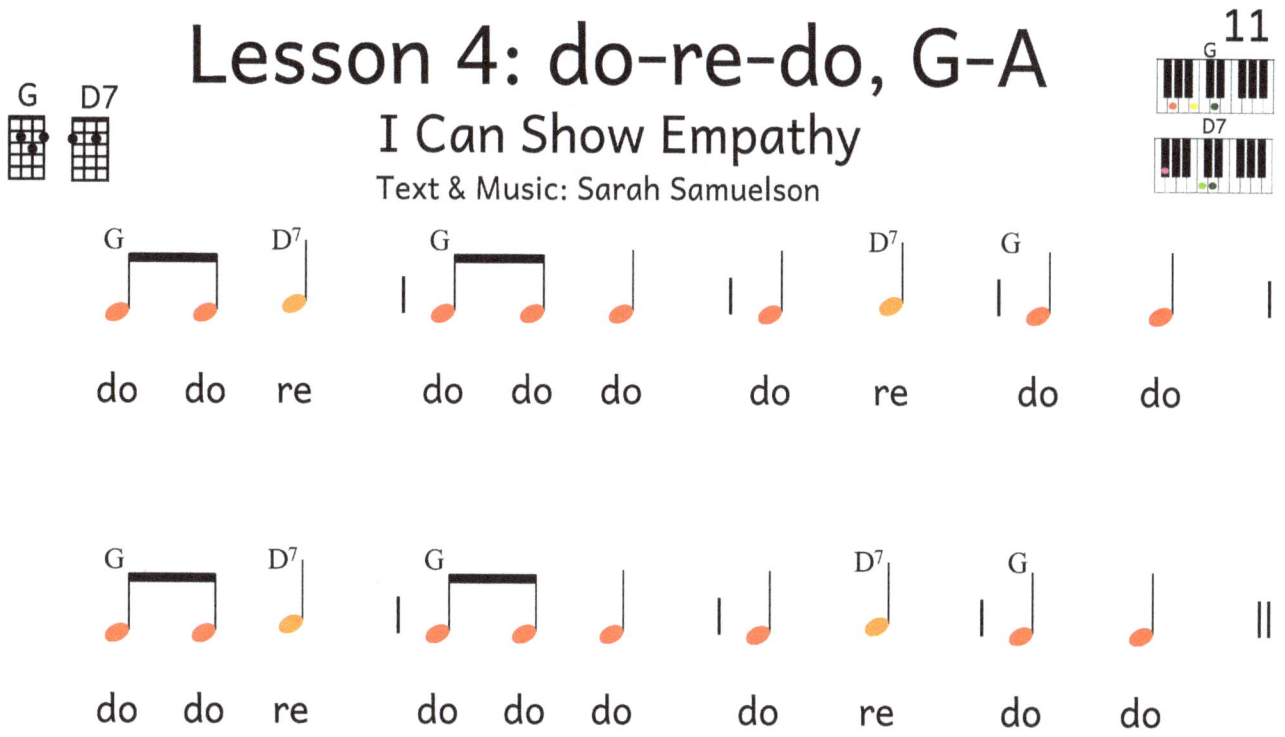

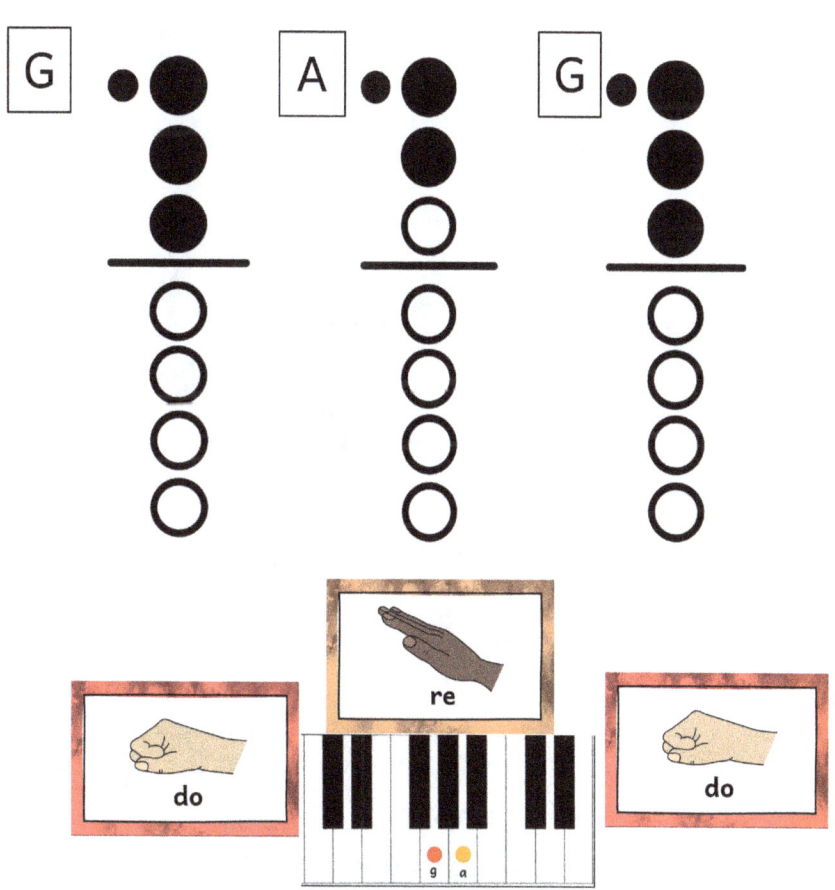

English
I Can Show Empathy
Text & Music: Sarah Samuelson

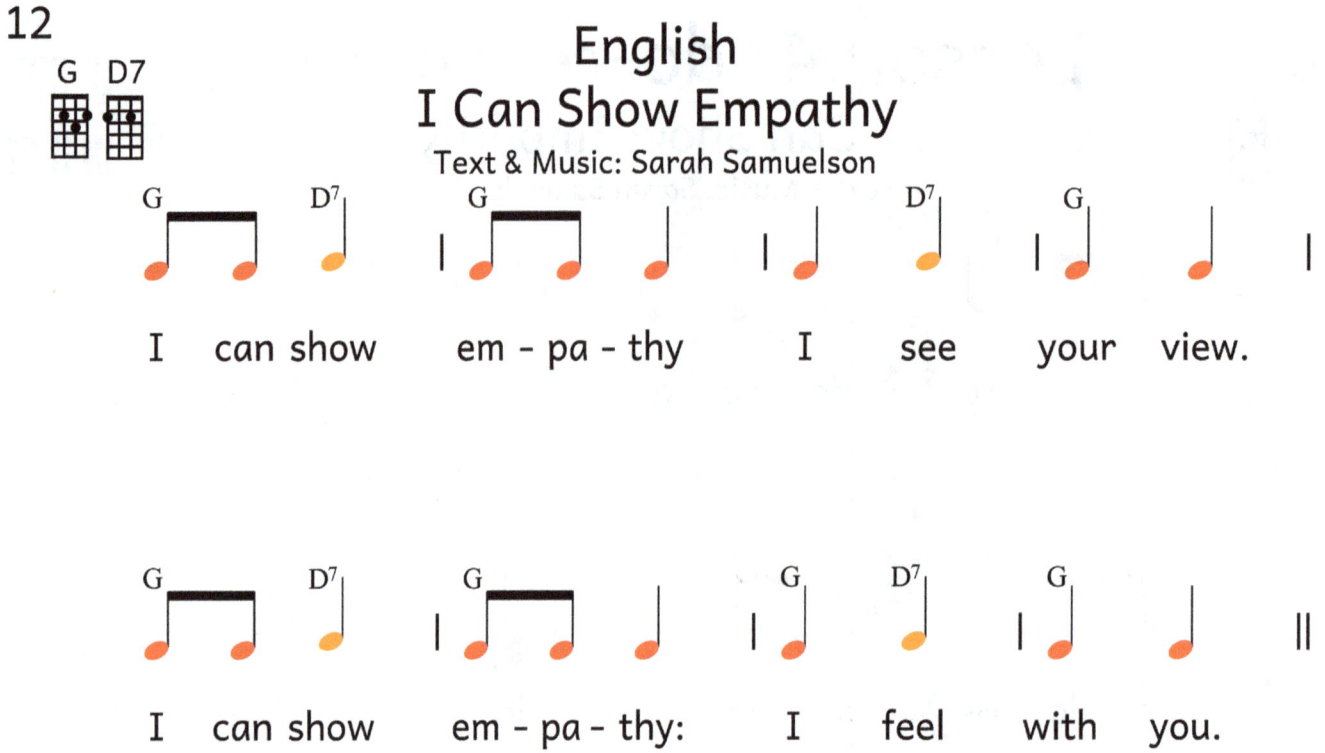

I can show em-pa-thy. I see your view.

I can show em-pa-thy: I feel with you.

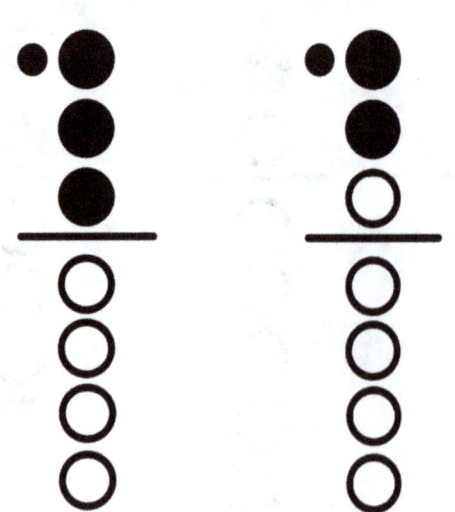

International Phonetic Alphabet
aɪ kæn ʃoʊ ˈɛmpəθi. aɪ si jʊr vjuː.
aɪ kæn ʃoʊ ˈɛmpəθi. aɪ fil wɪð jʊ

Copyright © 2024 Sarah Samuelson Studio

Español
Mostrar empatía
Music: Sarah Samuelson

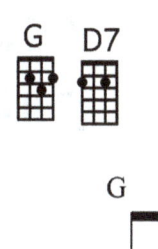

Mo-strar em-pa tí - a   Ve-o tu pun - to de vi-sta.

Mo-strar em - pa - tí - a   Sien-to con - ti - go.

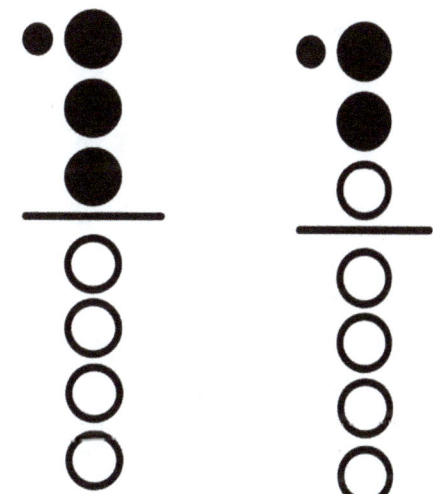

Español	International Phonetic Alphabet
Mostrar empatía.	mosˈtrar emˈpati.a
Veo tu punto de vista.	ˈbe.o tu ˈpunto de ˈbista
Mostrar empatía:	mosˈtrar emˈpati.a
Siento contigo.	ˈsjento konˈtiɣo

Copyright © 2024 Sarah Samuelson Studio

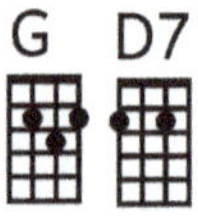

Lesson 5: do-re-mi, G-A-B
Do-Re-Mi Body Tap
Music: Sarah Samuelson

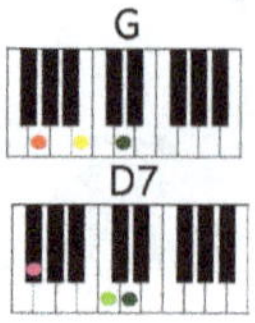

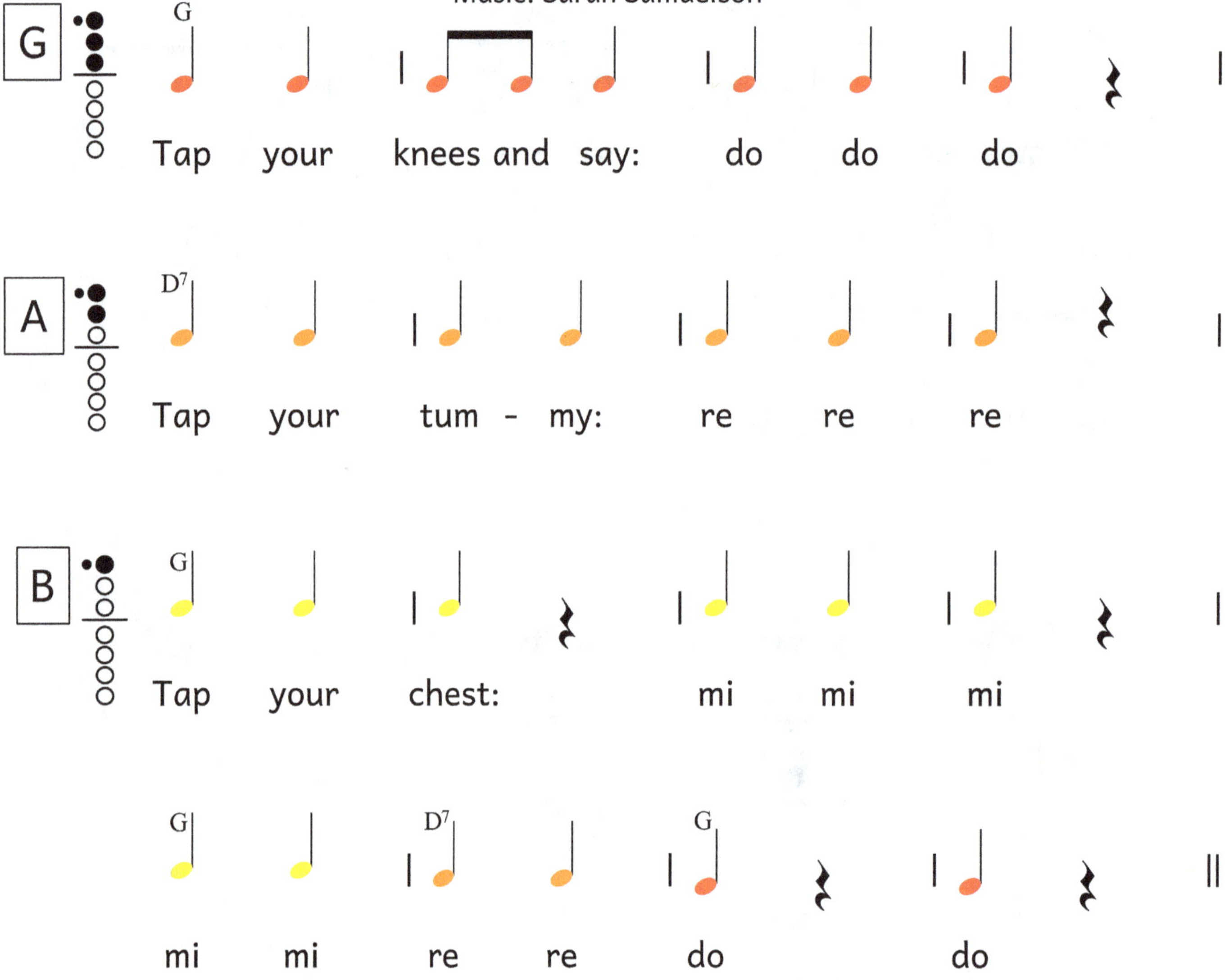

G: Tap your knees and say: do do do

A: Tap your tummy: re re re

B: Tap your chest: mi mi mi

mi mi re re do do

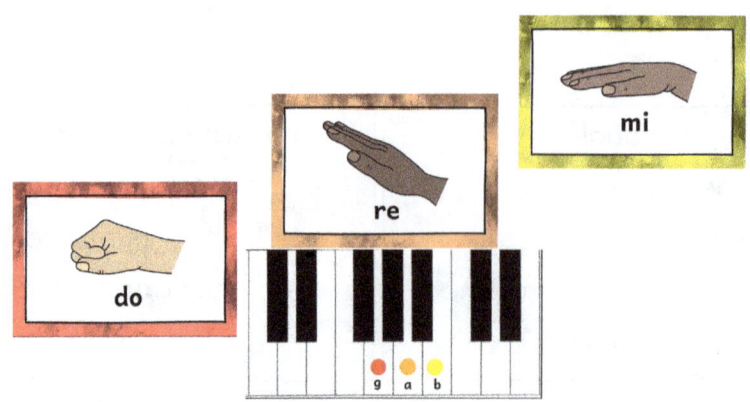

Copyright © 2024 Sarah Samuelson Studio

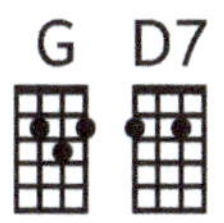

English
Words Can Be Healing to Say
Text & Music: Sarah Samuelson

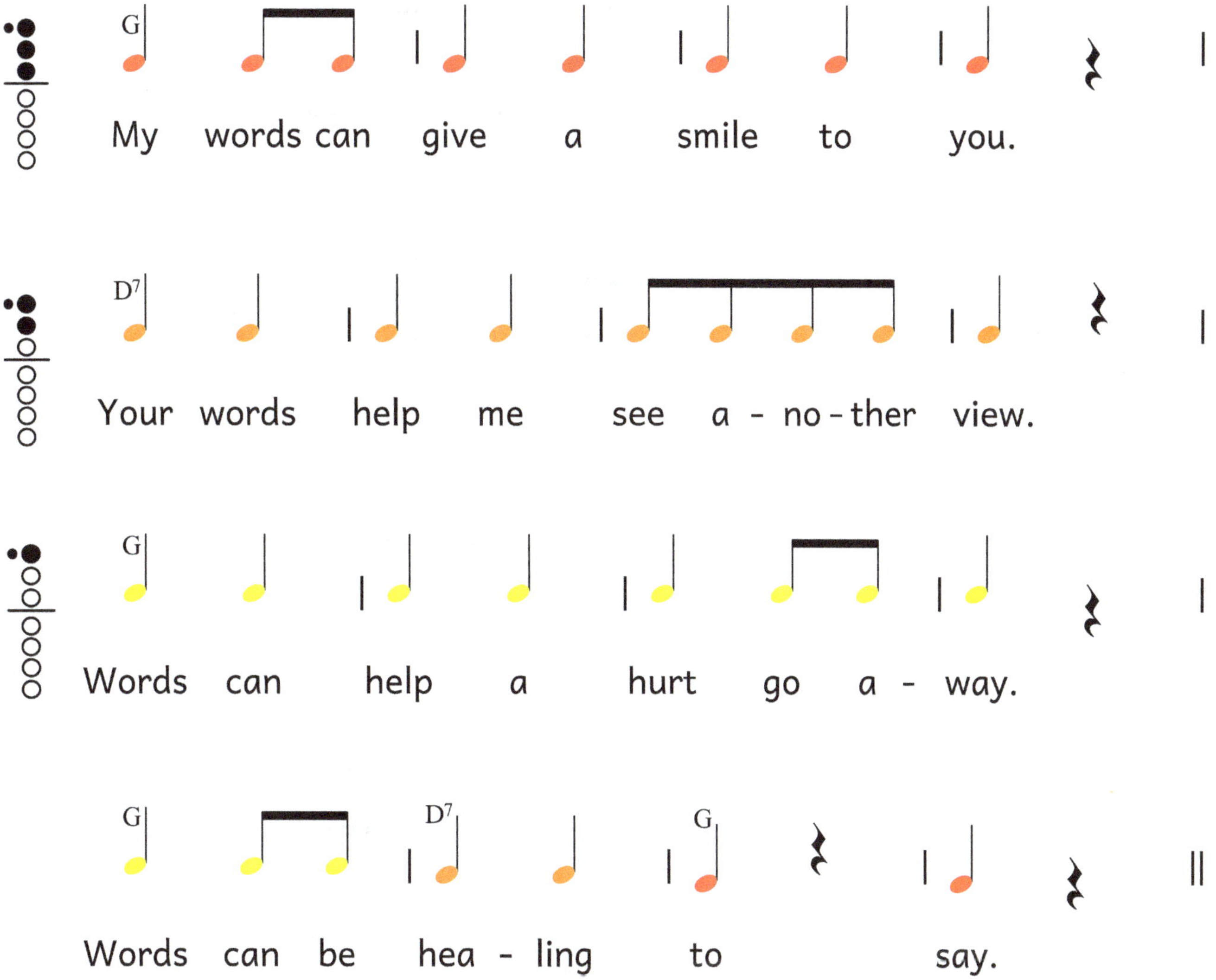

My words can give a smile to you.

Your words help me see a-no-ther view.

Words can help a hurt go a-way.

Words can be hea-ling to say.

International Phonetic Alphabet
mɪ wɜrdz kæn gɪv ə smaɪl tu ju
jur wɜrdz hɛlp mi si əˈnəðər vjuː
wɜrdz kæn hɛlp ə hɜrt goʊ əˈweɪ
wɜrdz kæn bi ˈhilɪŋ tu seɪ

Copyright © 2024 Sarah Samuelson Studio

Lesson 6: Five line staff
Welcome Here!
Music: English Round (Hot Cross Buns)

Notice that "do" which here is middle C, has a line through it to remind you that it is middle C. Can you find all of the middle Cs?

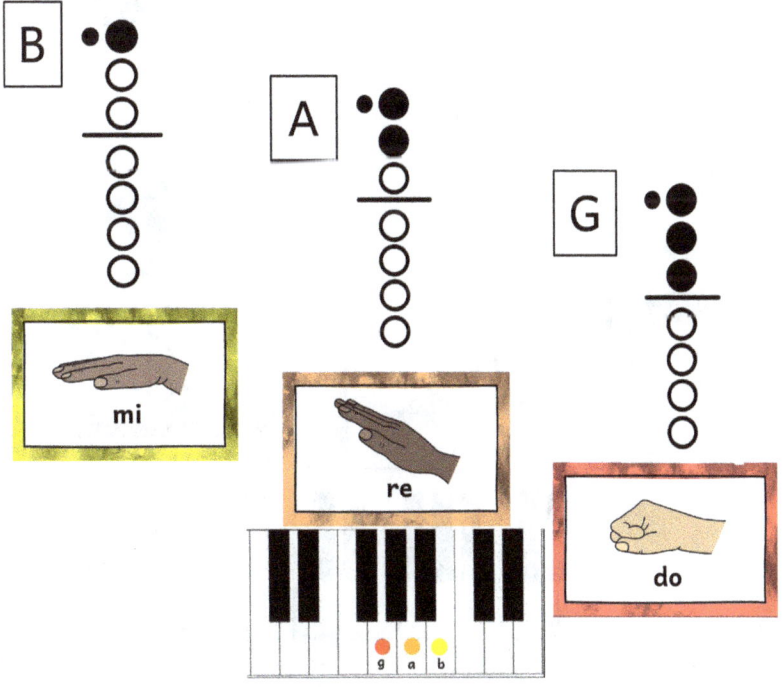

Copyright © 2024 Sarah Samuelson Studio

English Welcome Here!
Music: English Round (Hot Cross Buns)

mi re do do do mi re do
wi want ɔl tu fil ˈwɛl - kəm hɪr
We want all to feel wel - come here.

do do do do re re re re mi re do
wi ˈvæl - ju ðə ˈkʌl tʃər əv itʃ ˈpɜr sən - hɪr
We va - lue the cul - ture of each per - son here.

Notice that "do" which here is middle C, has a line through it since it is not on the 5-lines. This tune is a "round" which can be sung by two, three or four different people. The first person starts singing and when they get to the number 2, the second person starts and the same for the third and fourth person.

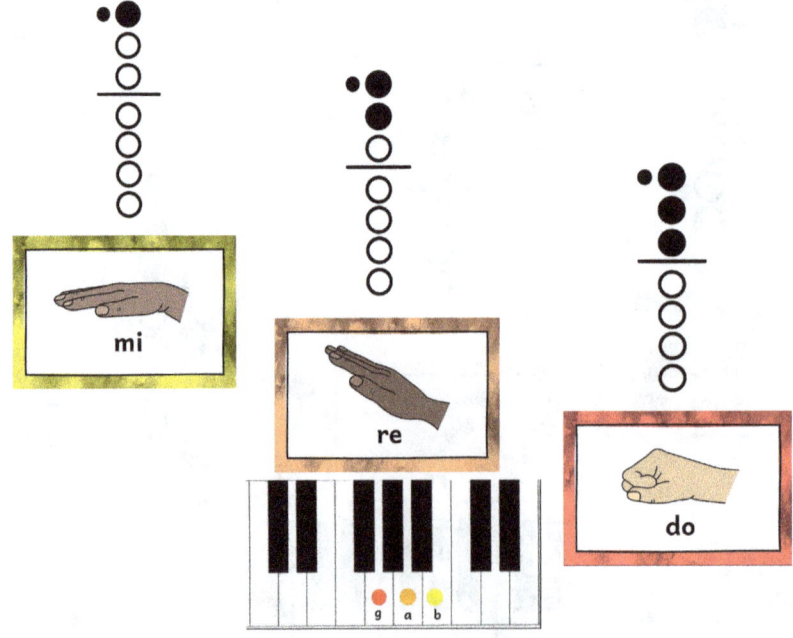

Copyright © 2024 Sarah Samuelson Studio

Español
Bienvenido aquí
Music: English Round (Hot Cross Buns)

19

ke - ˈre - mos ke   ˈto-ðos se sjen - ˈtan bjen - ˈbe - ni   -ðos a - ˈki
Que-re-mos que   to-dos se sien-tan bien-ven-i - dos a-quí

βa - lor - ˈa -mos   ˈla kul-ˈtu - ra   de ˈka-ða per - ˈso - na   a - ˈki
Va-lor-a-mos   la cul-tu-ra   de ca-da per - so-na   a-quí.

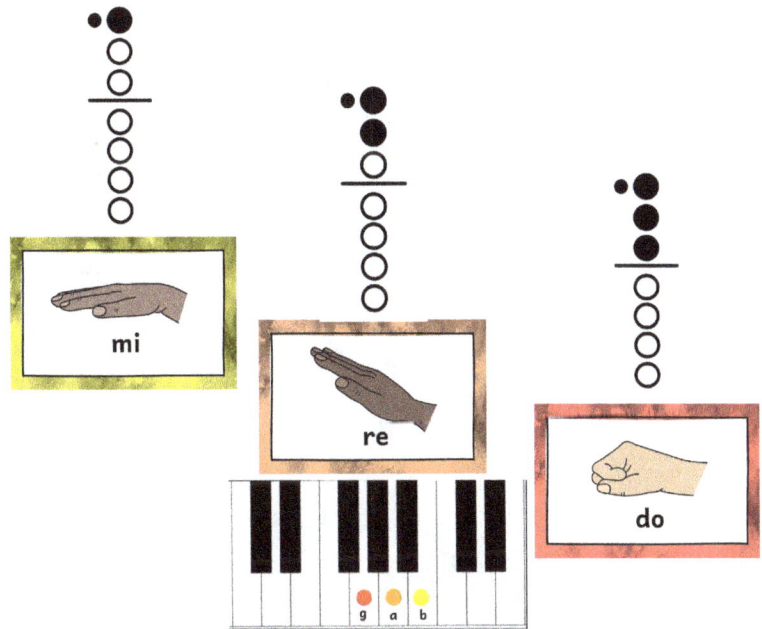

Español	International Phonetic Alphabet
Queremos que todos se sientan bienvenidos aquí	keˈremos ke ˈtoðos se ˈsjentan bjenˈbenidos aˈki
Valoramos la cultura de cada persona aquí	ba.loˈra.mos la kulˈtu.ra de ˈka.ða perˈso.na aˈki

Copyright © 2024 Sarah Samuelson Studio

Lesson 7: do-mi, G-B
I Can Be a Friend
Music: France (Au Clair de la Lune)

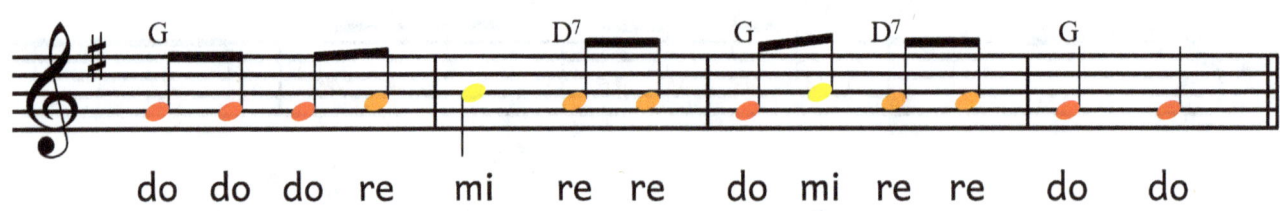

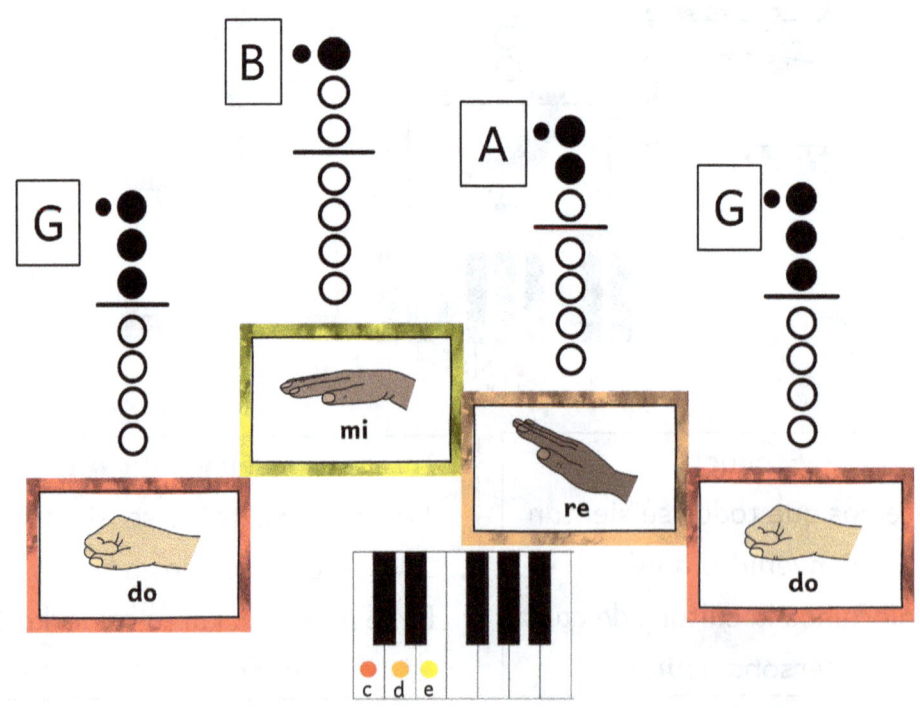

Copyright © 2024 Sarah Samuelson Studio

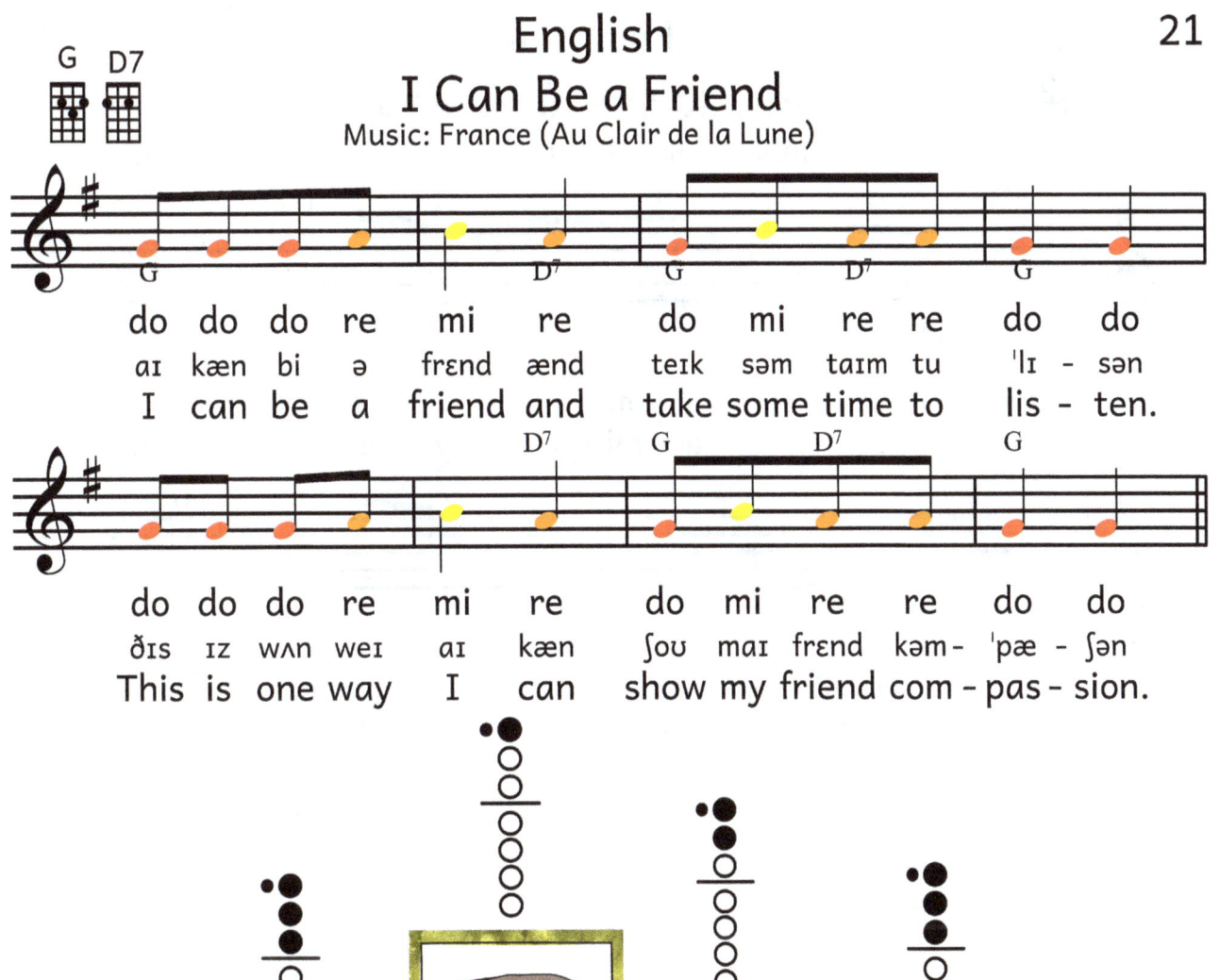

Traditional French:

o klɛr də la ly nə mõ na mi pjɛ ro
Au clair de la lune mon ami Pierrot

prɛ tə mwa ta ply mə pu re kri rœ̃ mo
Prête moi ta plume pour écrire un mot.

English Version:

In the moonlight my friend Pierrot,

lend me your pen to write a word.

Copyright © 2024 Sarah Samuelson Studio

Español
Puedo ser un amigo
Music: France (Au Clair de la Lune)

ˈpwe do ser un a-ˈmi ɣo i es-ku-ˈtʃar-te
Pue do ser un a-mi-go y es-cu-char-te.

ˈpwe do mo-ˈstrar kom-pa-ˈsjon a mi a-ˈmi-ɣo
Pue-do mo-strar com-pa-sión a mi a - mi - go.

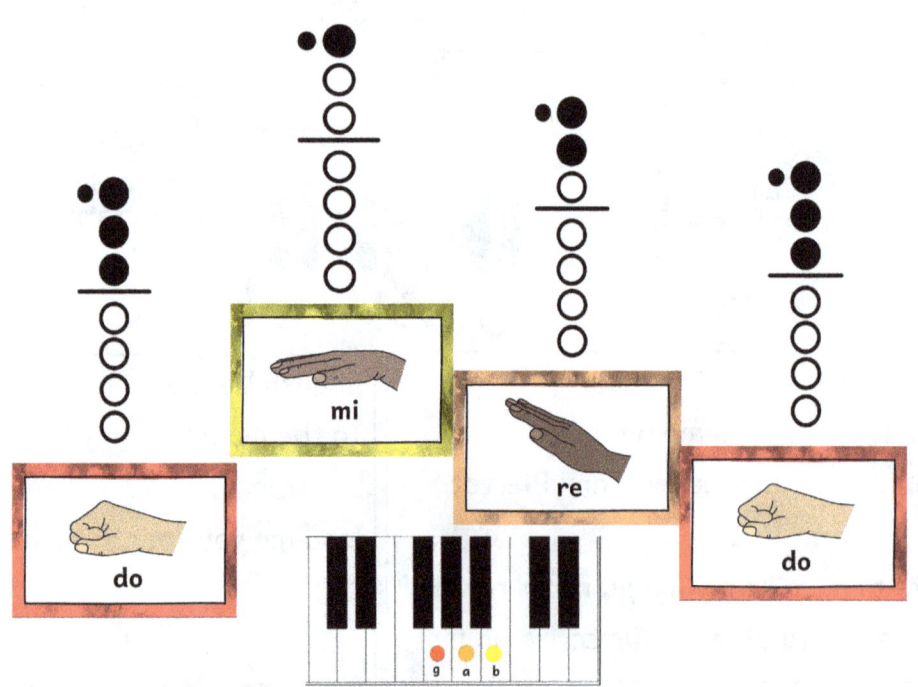

Copyright © 2024 Sarah Samuelson Studio

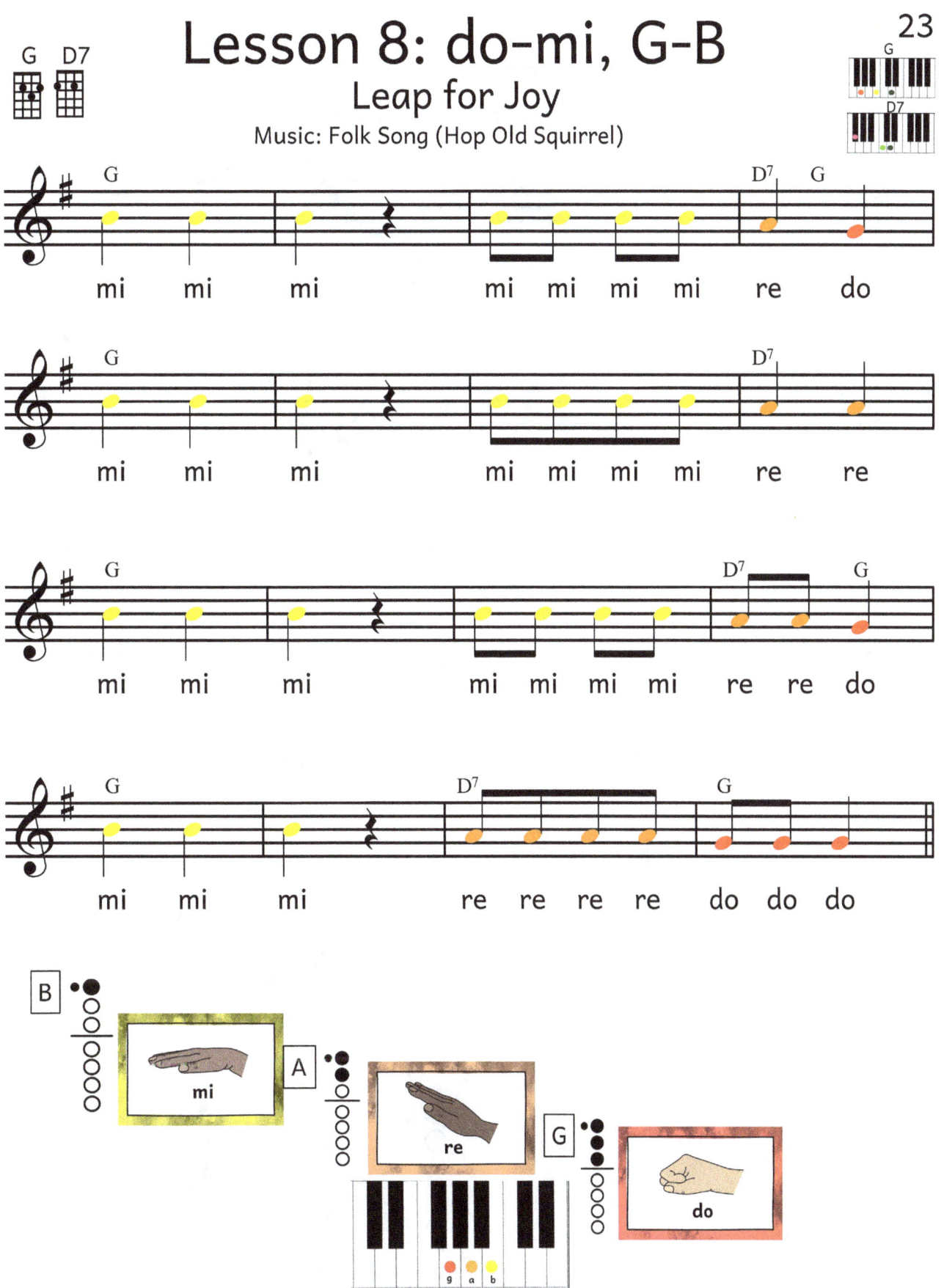

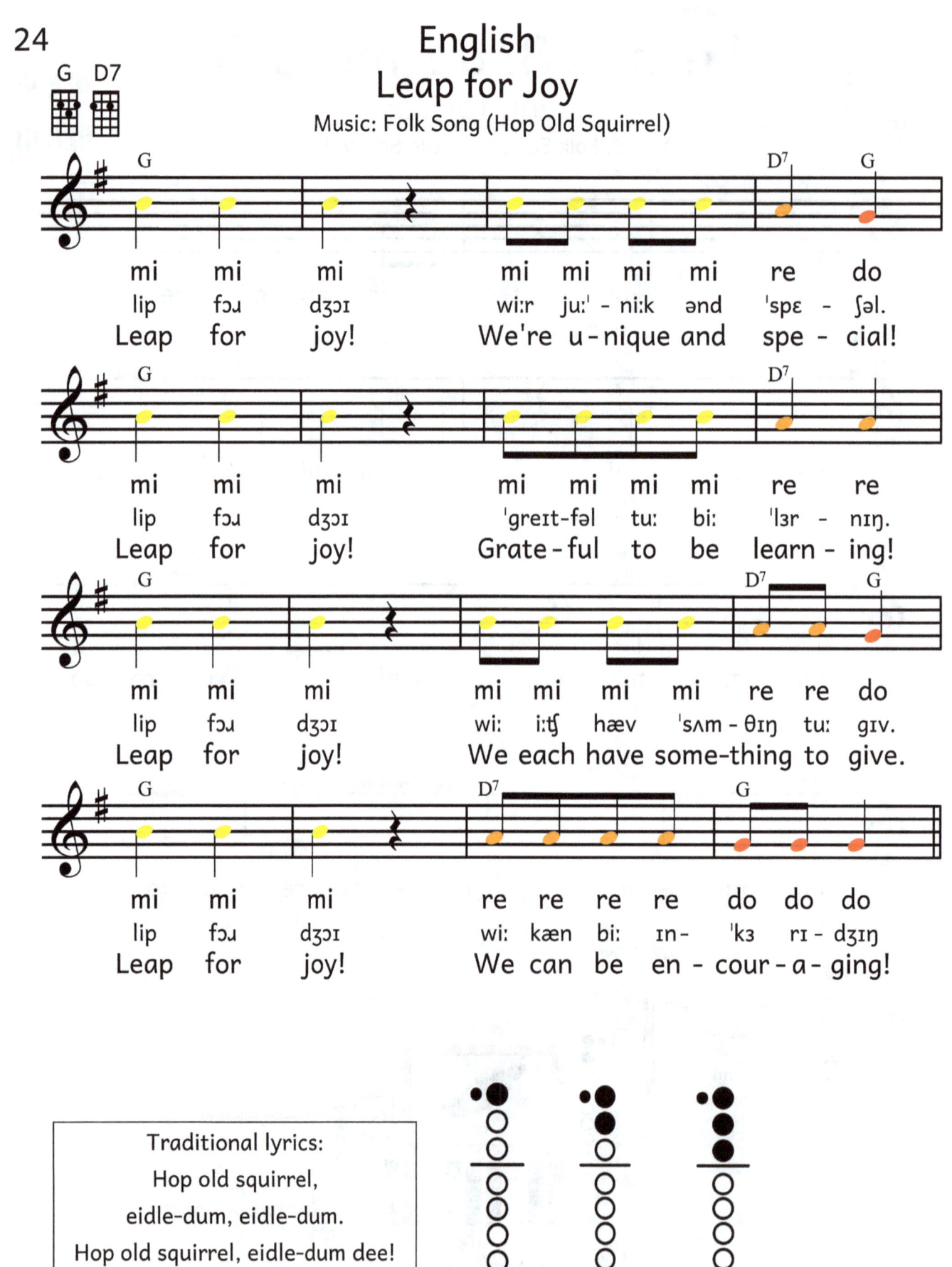

Español
Salta de alegría
Music: Folk Song (Hop Old Squirrel)

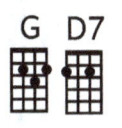

'sal - ta de a - le - 'gri - a 'so mos es - pe - 'sja - les
Sal - ta de a - le - grí - a So - mos es - pe - cia - les.

'sal tar de a - le - 'gri - a gra - sjas por a - pren - 'der
Sal ter de a - le - grí - a, gra - cias por a - pren - der.

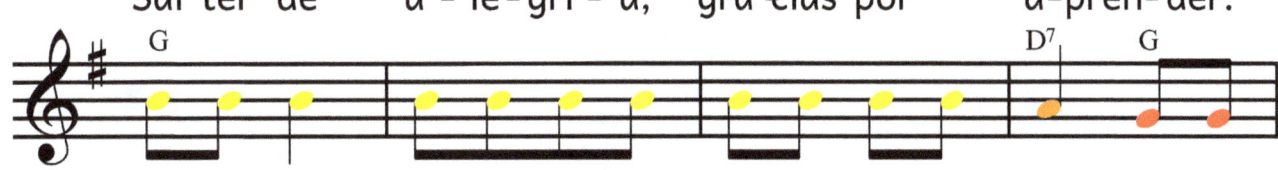

'sal ta de a - le - 'gri - a ka - ða 'u - no ða 'al - go
Sal ta de a - le - grí - a, Ca - do u - no da al - go.

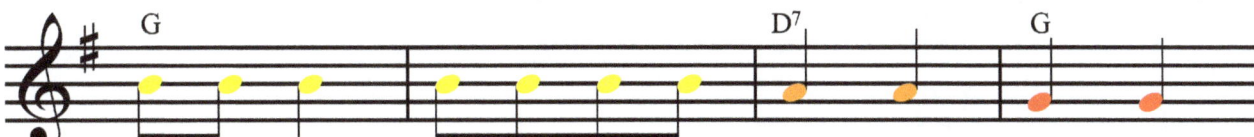

'sal - ta de a - le - 'gri - a a - ni - ma - mos
Sal ta de a - le - grí - a, a - ni - ma - mos

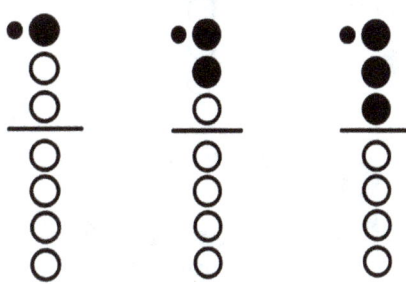

Copyright © 2024 Sarah Samuelson Studio

Lesson 9: do-mi, G-B
I Can Be More Understanding
Music: African American Spiritual (Babylon's Falling)

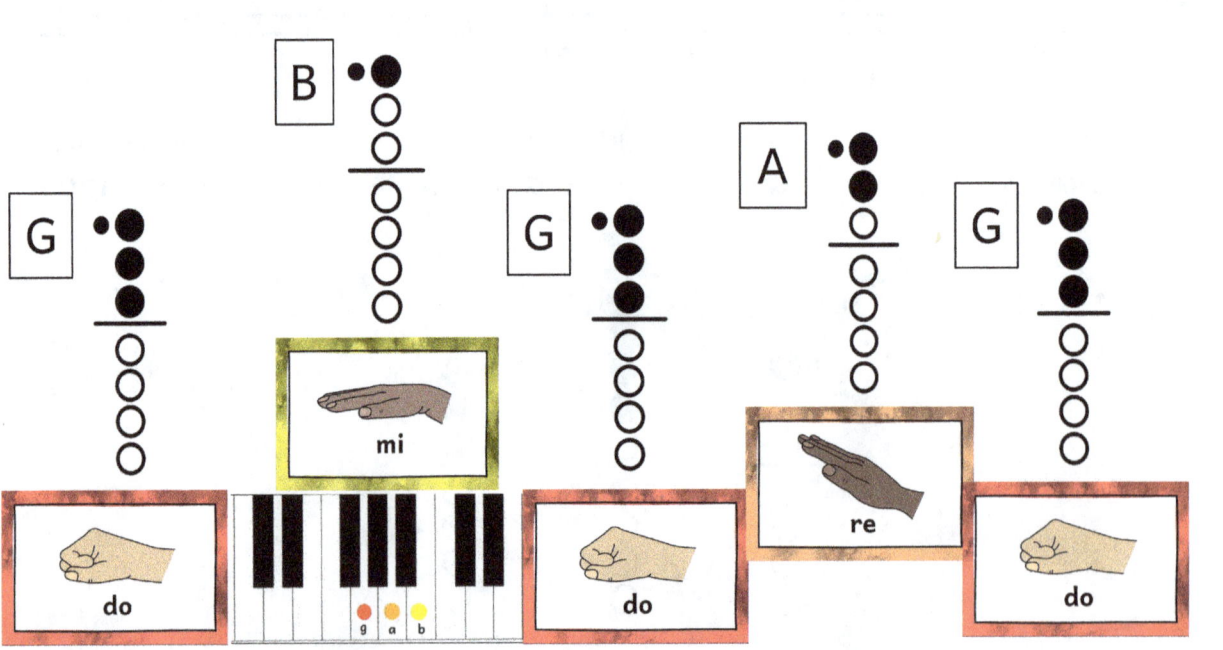

Copyright © 2024 Sarah Samuelson Studio

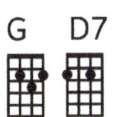

English
I Can Be More Understanding

Music: African American Spiritual (Babylon's Falling)

do do mi do re do do mi do
aɪ kæn lɜrn tə salv ˈmɛ - ni ˈpra - bləmz
I can learn to solve ma - ny pro - blems.

do do mi do re re do do
aɪ kæn bi mɔr ʌn - dər - ˈstæn - dɪŋ
I can be more un - der - stand - ing

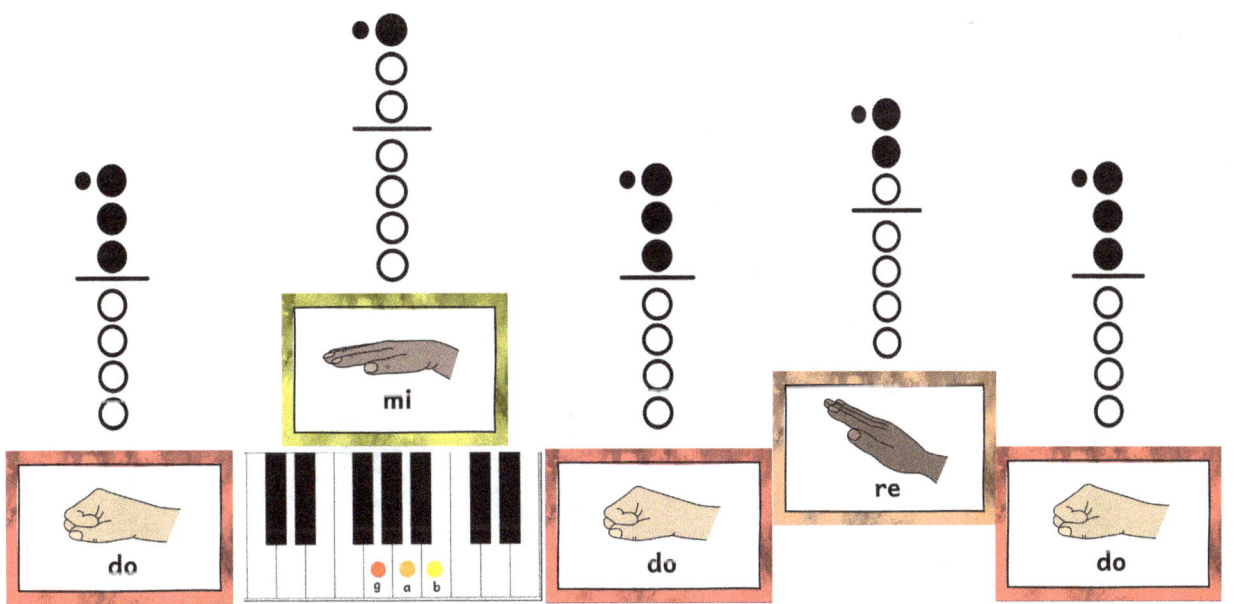

Traditional lyrics:
Babylon's falling, falling, falling,
Babylon's falling to rise no more.
Listen to: Golden Gate Quartet sing "Babylon's Falling"

Copyright © 2024 Sarah Samuelson Studio

28

Español
Puedo ser más comprensivo
Music: African American Spiritual (Babylon's Falling)

ˈpwe-do a-pren-ˈder a re-sol-ˈβer pro-ble-mas
Pue-do a-pren-der a re-sol-ver pro-ble-mas.

ˈpwe ðo ser mas kom-pren-ˈsi-βo
Pue-do ser más com-pren-si-vo(a)

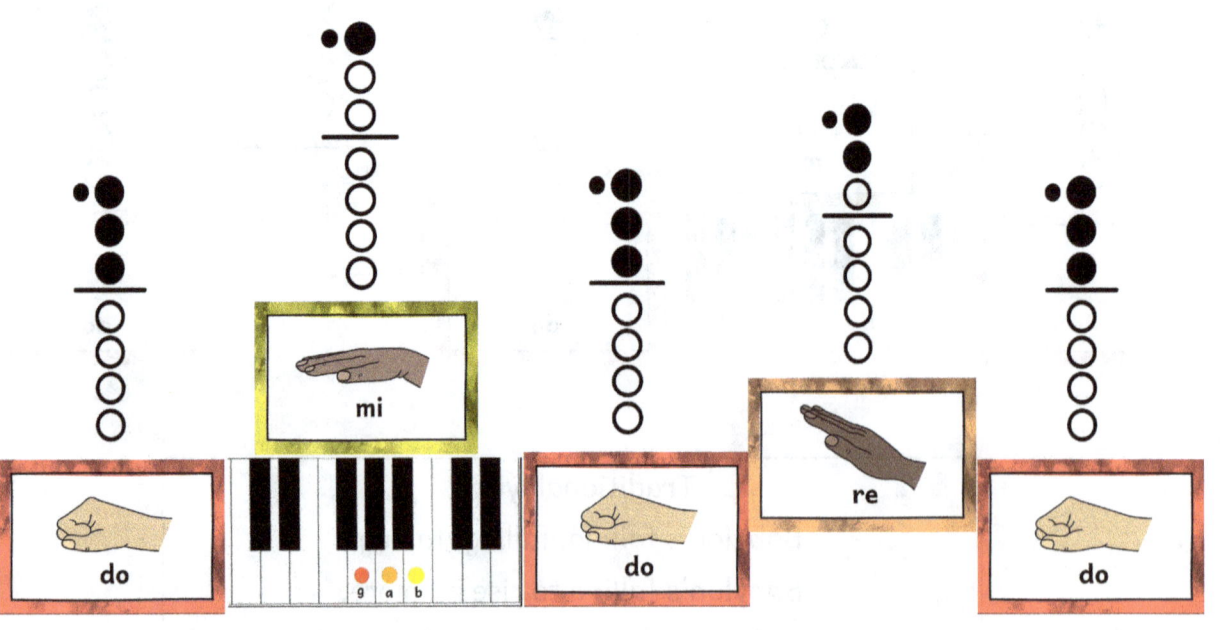

Copyright © 2024 Sarah Samuelson Studio

Lesson 10: NEW half note, so

Put Yourself in Their Shoes
Text: Danielle Coke Balfour; Music: Spiritual (Oh, I'm Goin' to Sing)

so mi mi mi mi re re re re do do do

re re re re mi mi so mi re do

> Treble clef is also called G Clef and shows where G is on the 5-line staff. This G is "so."
> Notice the curly part of the clef looks like a G.

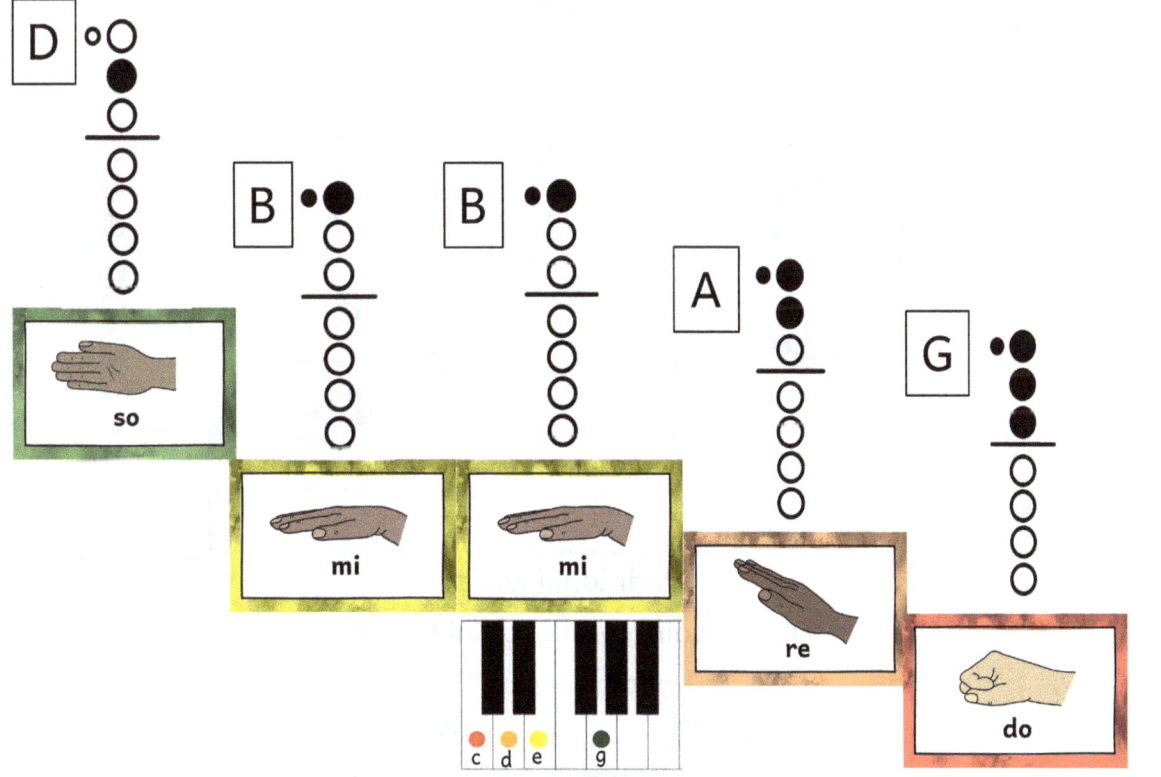

Copyright © 2024 Sarah Samuelson Studio

English
Put Yourself in Their Shoes

Text: Danielle Coke Balfour; Music: Spiritual (Oh, I'm Goin' to Sing)

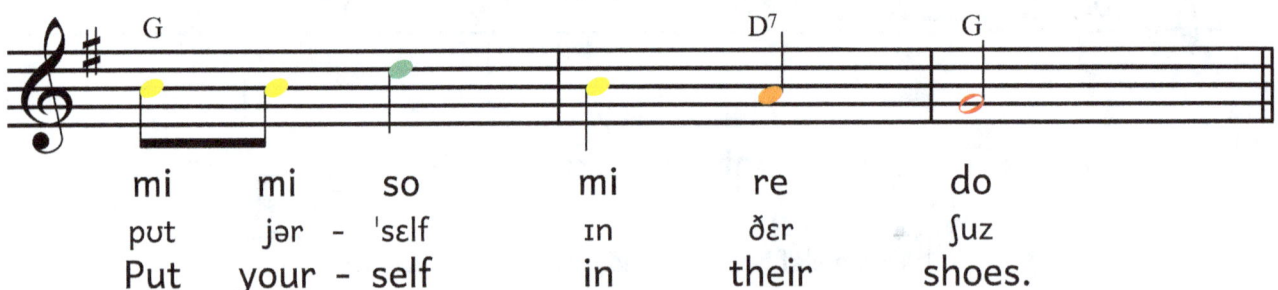

Traditional lyrics:
Oh I'm goin' to sing, goin' to sing,
goin' to sing
goin' to sing along my way.

Copyright © 2024 Sarah Samuelson Studio

Español
Ponte en su Lugar

Music: African American Spiritual (Oh, I'm Goin' to Sing)

ˈno de-βe-ˈri-a su-θer-ˈder-te pa-ra im-por ˈtar-te
"No de-be-rí-a su-ce-der-te pa-ra im-por-tar-te

ˈpon te en su lu - ˈɣar
Pon - te en su lu - gar.

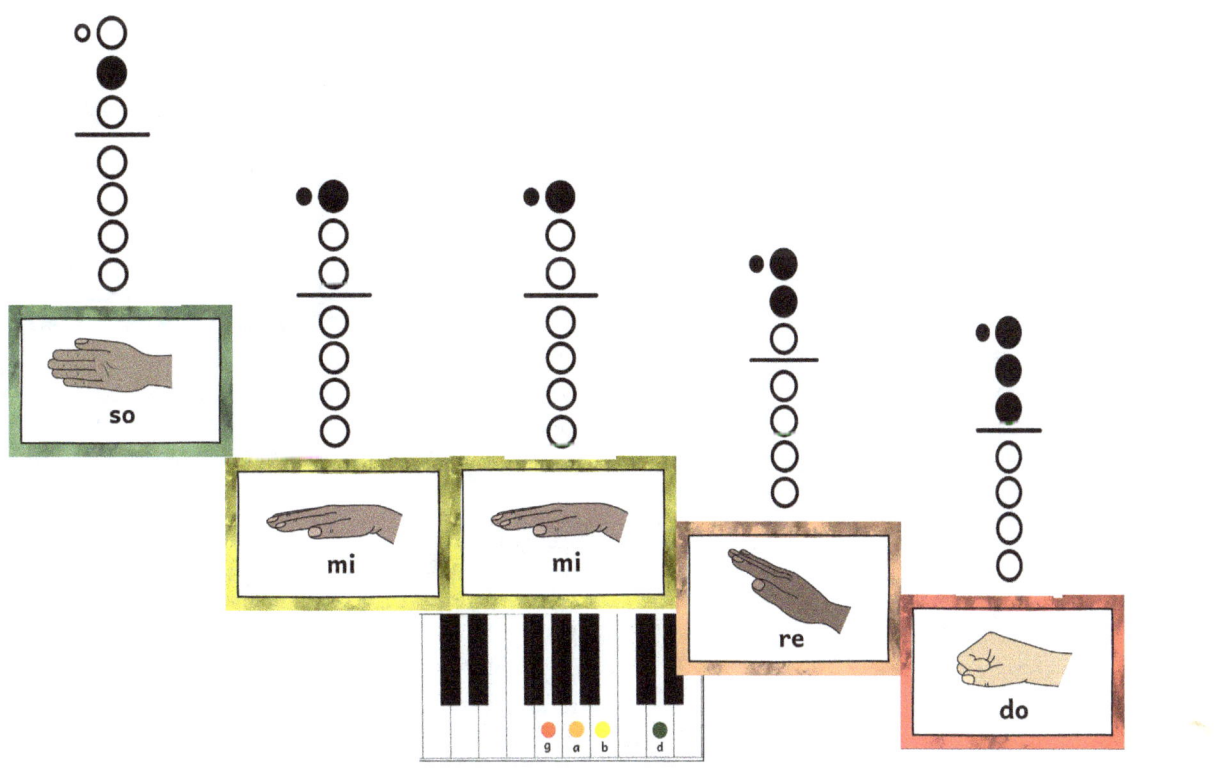

Copyright © 2024 Sarah Samuelson Studio

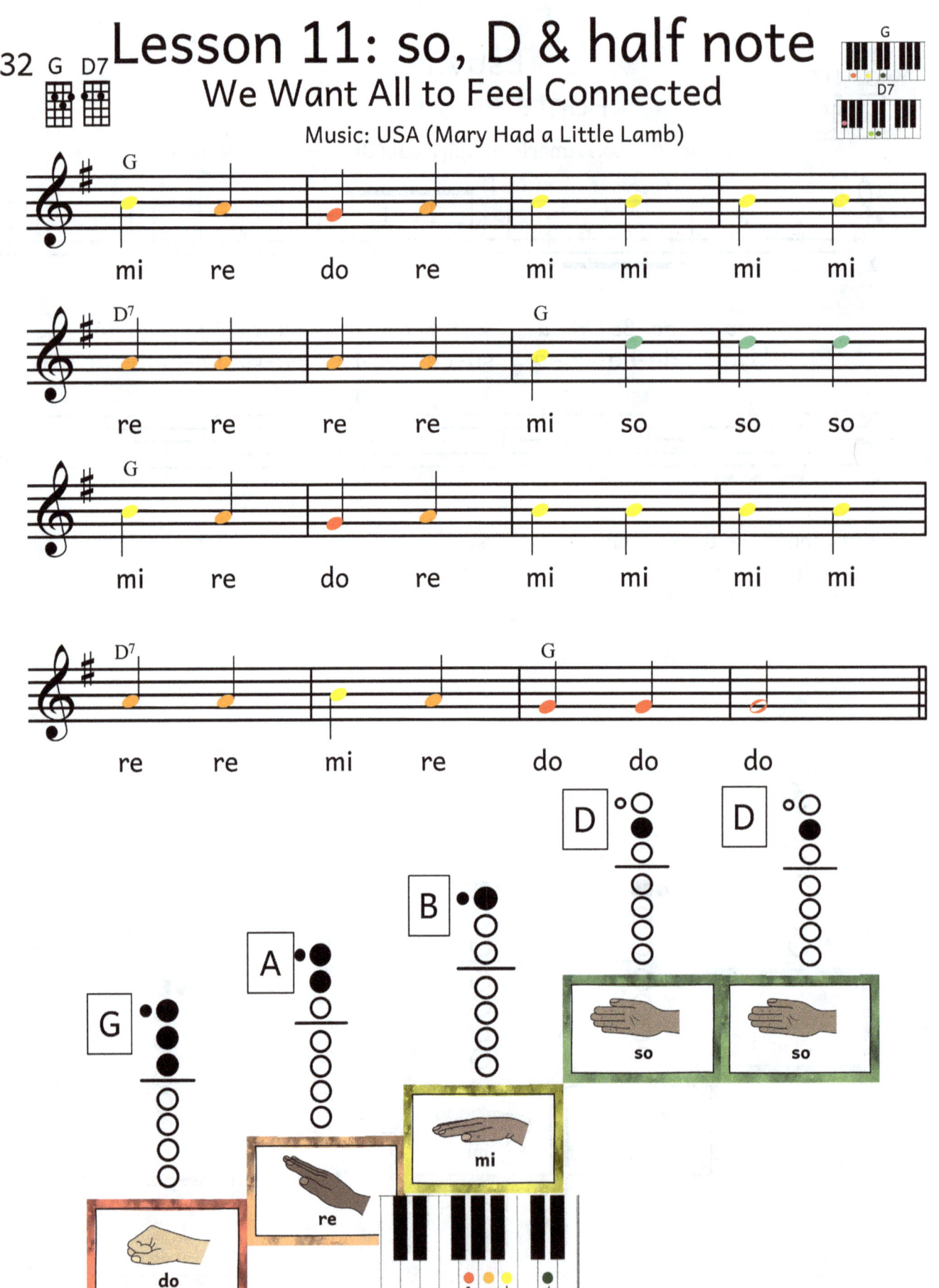

English

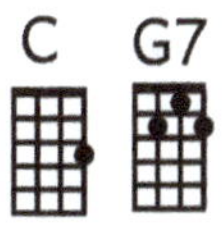

We Want All to Feel Connected

Music: USA (Mary Had a Little Lamb)

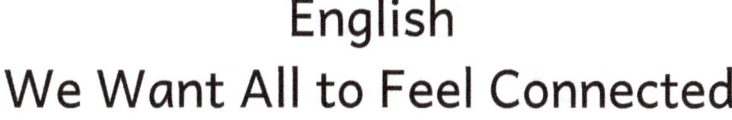

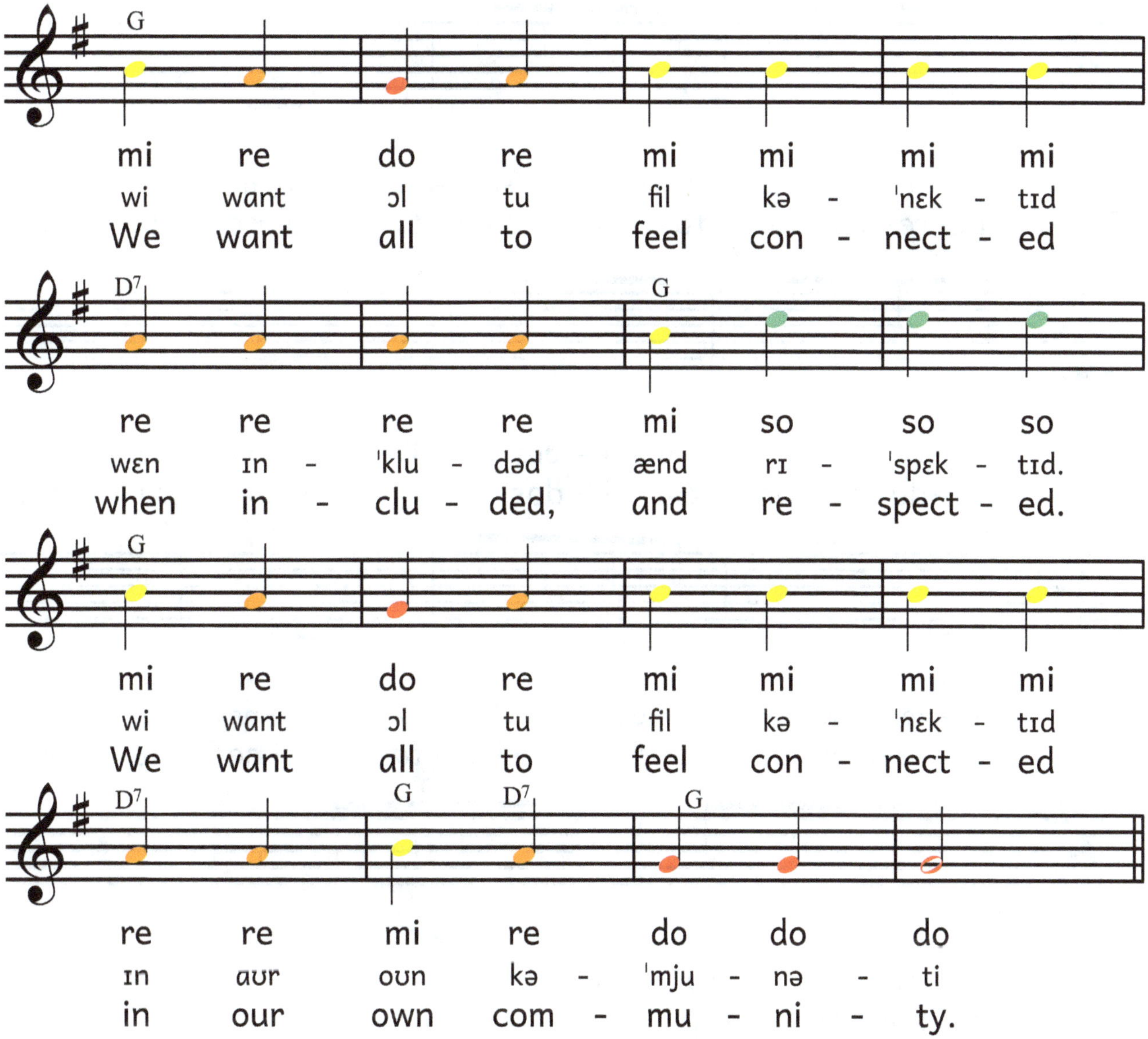

Traditional lyrics:
Mary had a little lamb, little lamb, little lamb, Mary had a little lamb
it's fleece was white as snow.

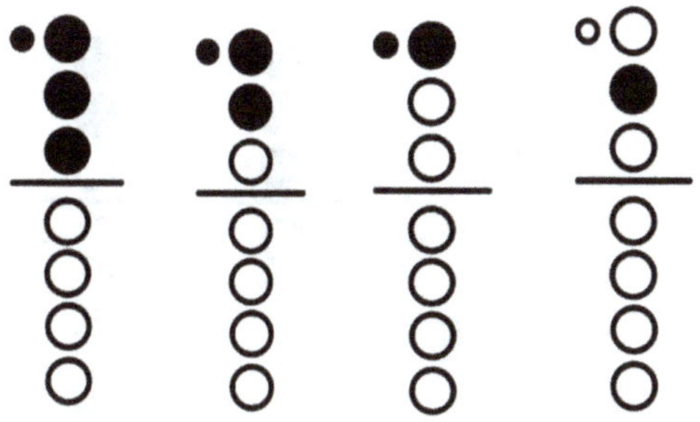

Español
Queremos ke todos se sientan conectados
Music: USA (Mary Had a Little Lamb)

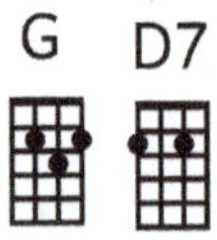

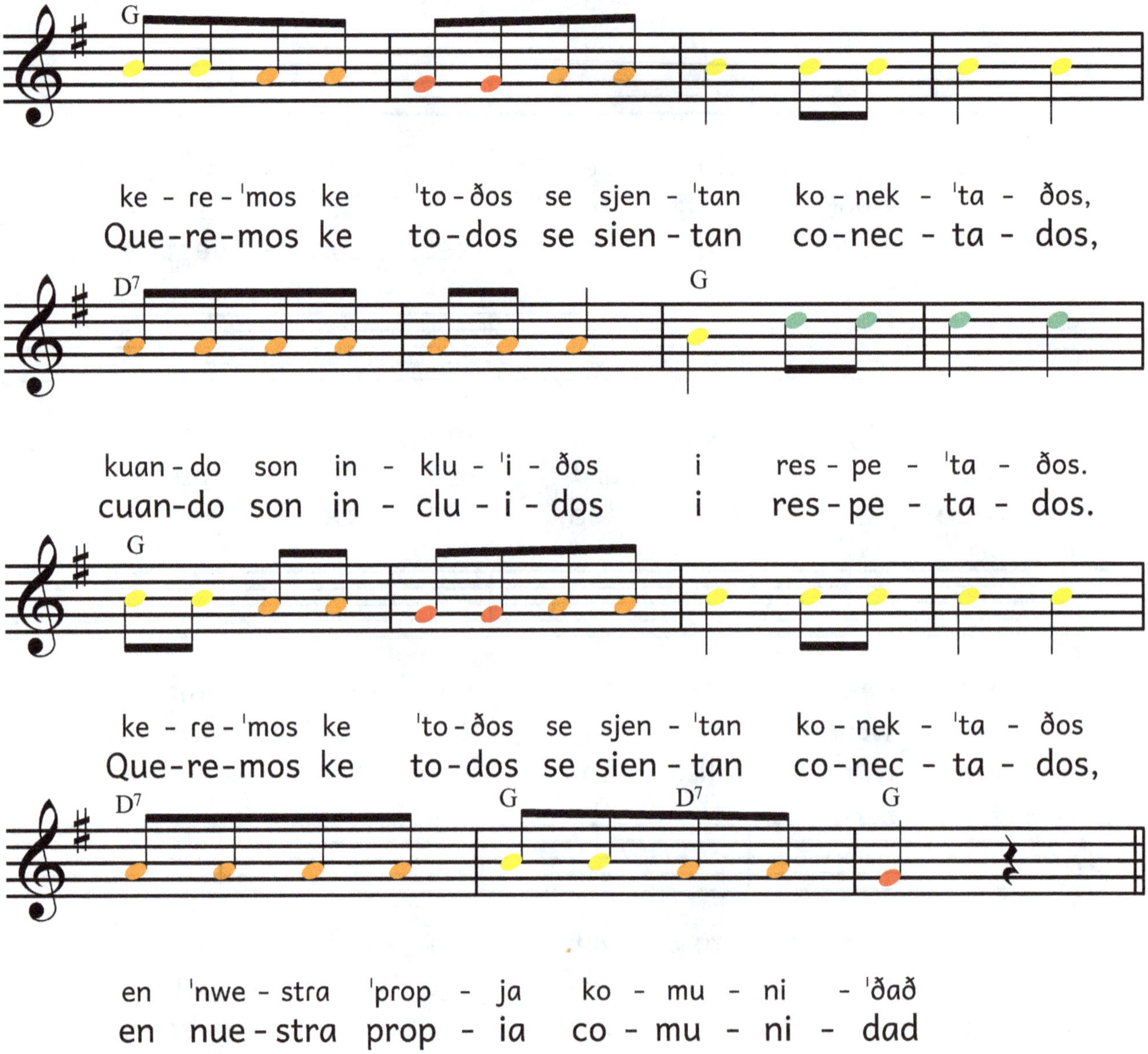

ke - re - 'mos ke 'to - ðos se sjen - 'tan ko - nek - 'ta - ðos,
Que-re-mos ke to-dos se sien - tan co-nec - ta - dos,

kuan - do son in - klu - 'i - ðos i res - pe - 'ta - ðos.
cuan-do son in - clu - i - dos i res - pe - ta - dos.

ke - re - 'mos ke 'to - ðos se sjen - 'tan ko - nek - 'ta - ðos
Que-re-mos ke to-dos se sien - tan co-nec - ta - dos,

en 'nwe - stra 'prop - ja ko - mu - ni - 'ðað
en nue - stra prop - ia co - mu - ni - dad

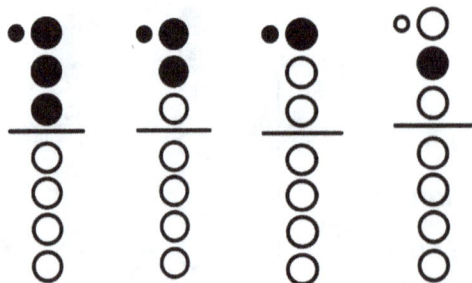

Copyright © 2024 Sarah Samuelson Studio

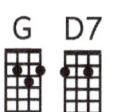

Lesson 12: LEAP, re-so
We Each Have a Family
Music: USA (Johnny Works with One Hammer)

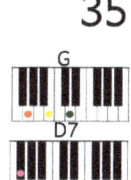

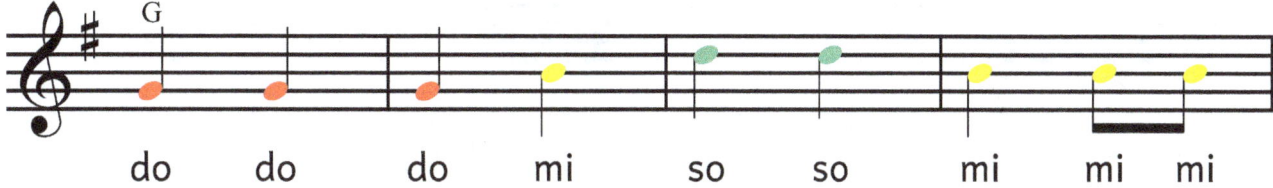

do do do mi so so mi mi mi

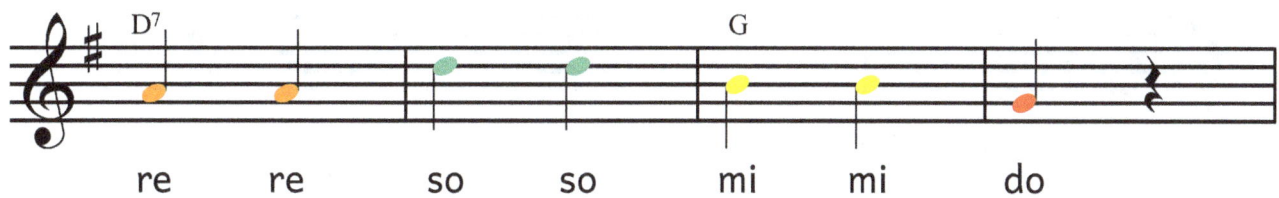

re re so so mi mi do

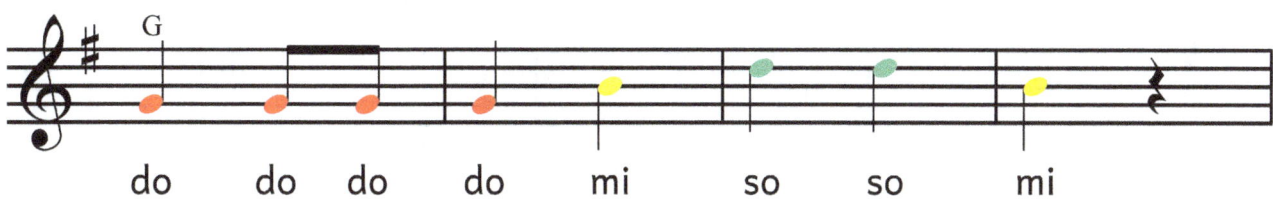

do do do do mi so so mi

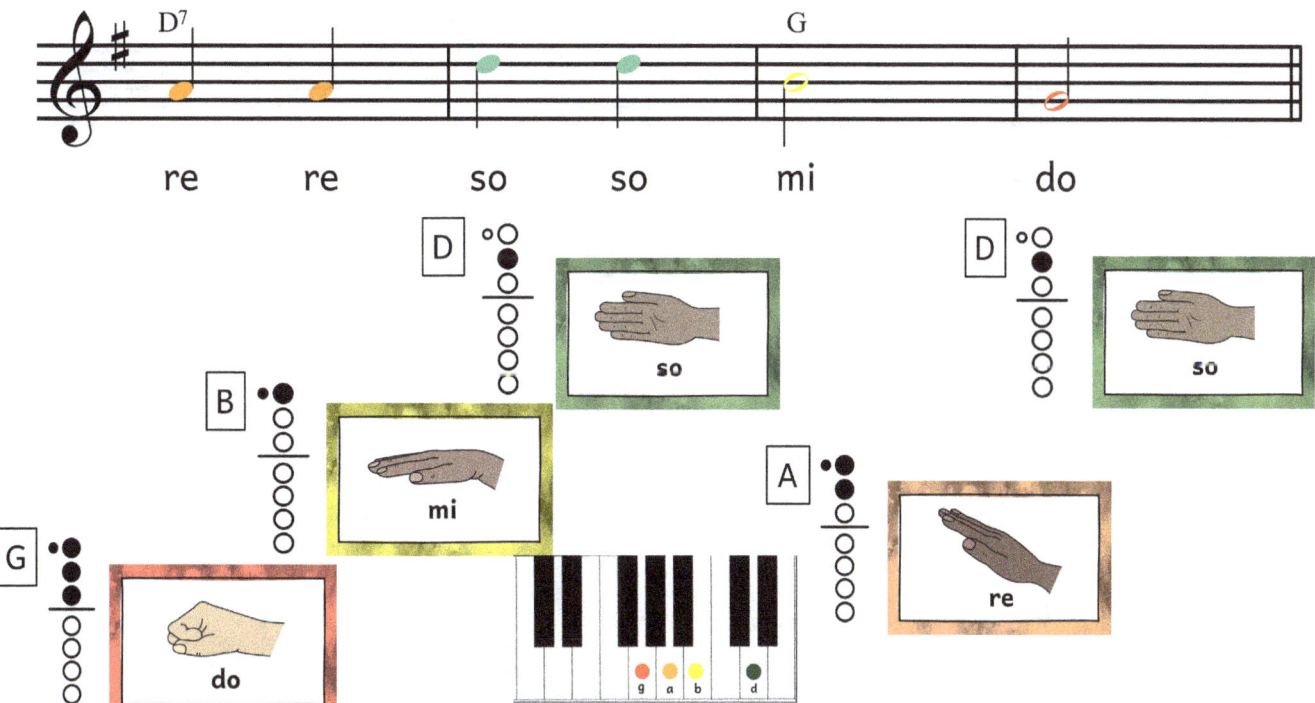

re re so so mi do

Copyright © 2024 Sarah Samuelson Studio

Español
Cado Uno Tiene Una Familia
Music: USA (Johnny Works with One Hammer)

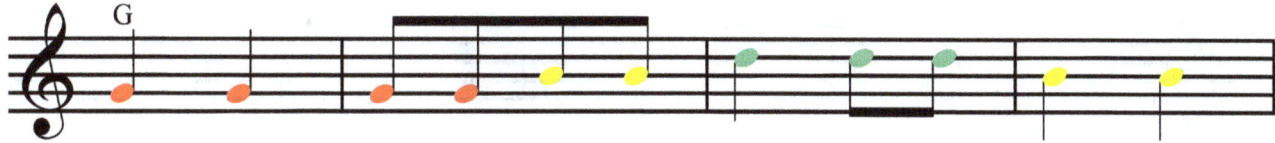

ˈka - ðo   ˈu - no tje - ne   u - na fa - ˈmil - ja
Ca - do   u - no   tie - ne   u - na fa - mil - ia,

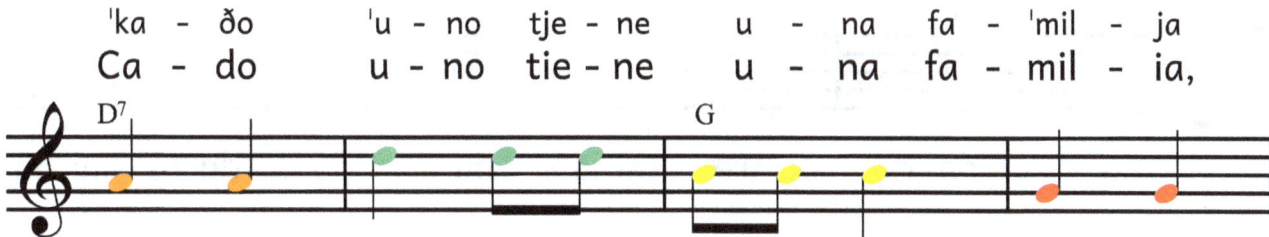

tra - ði - ˈsjo - nes, kul - ˈtu - ra, i - ˈdjo - mas.
tra - di - cio - nes, cul - tu - ra, i - dio - mas.

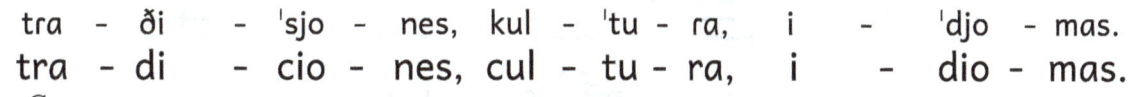

ˈa - blar de ˈnues - tras fa - ˈmil - jas nos a - ˈju - da
Ha - blar de nue stras fa - mi - lias nos a - yu - da

a sen - ˈtir - nos co nek - ˈta - dos
a sen - tir - nos   co - nec - ta - dos.

Copyright © 2024 Sarah Samuelson Studio

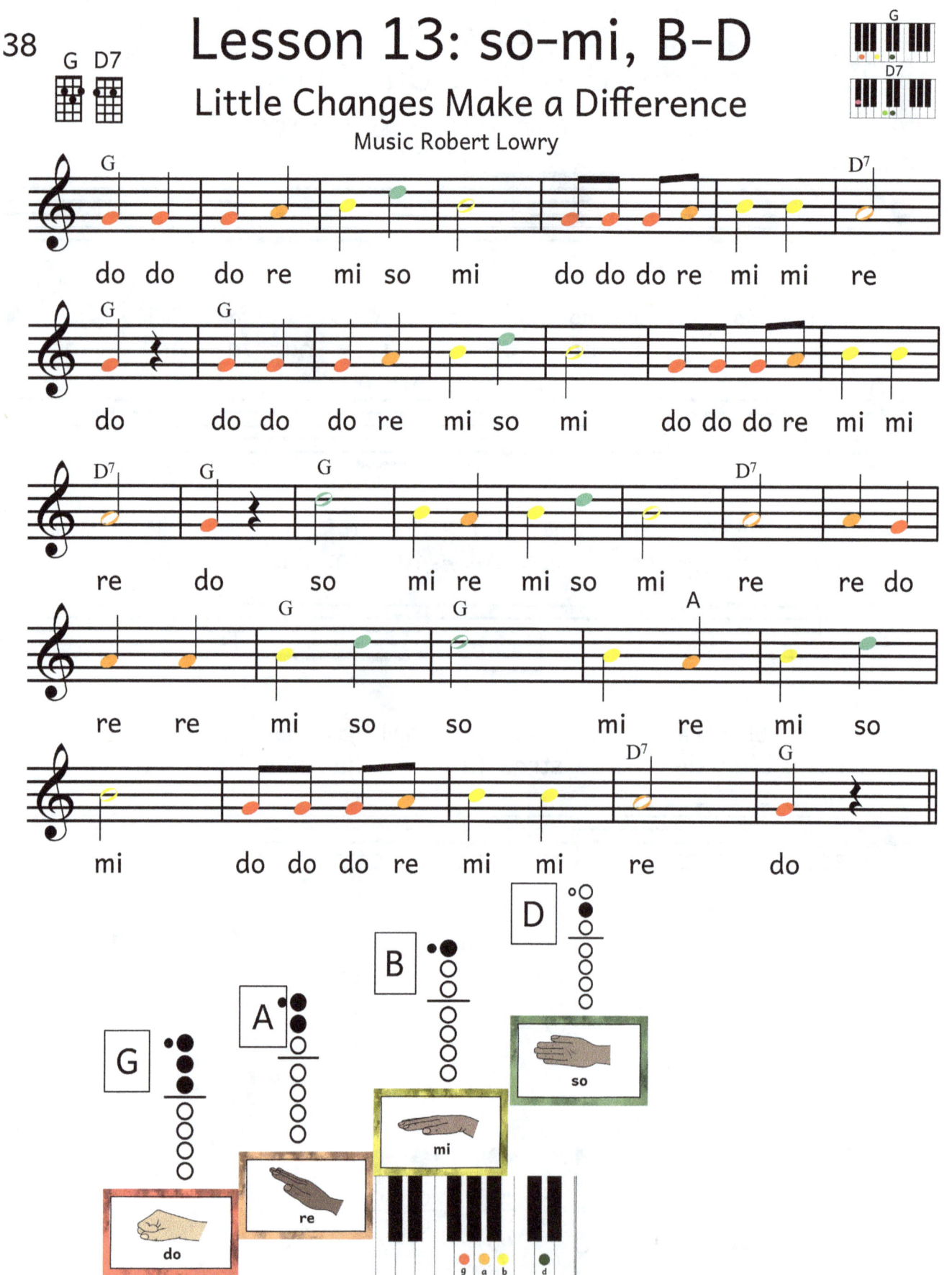

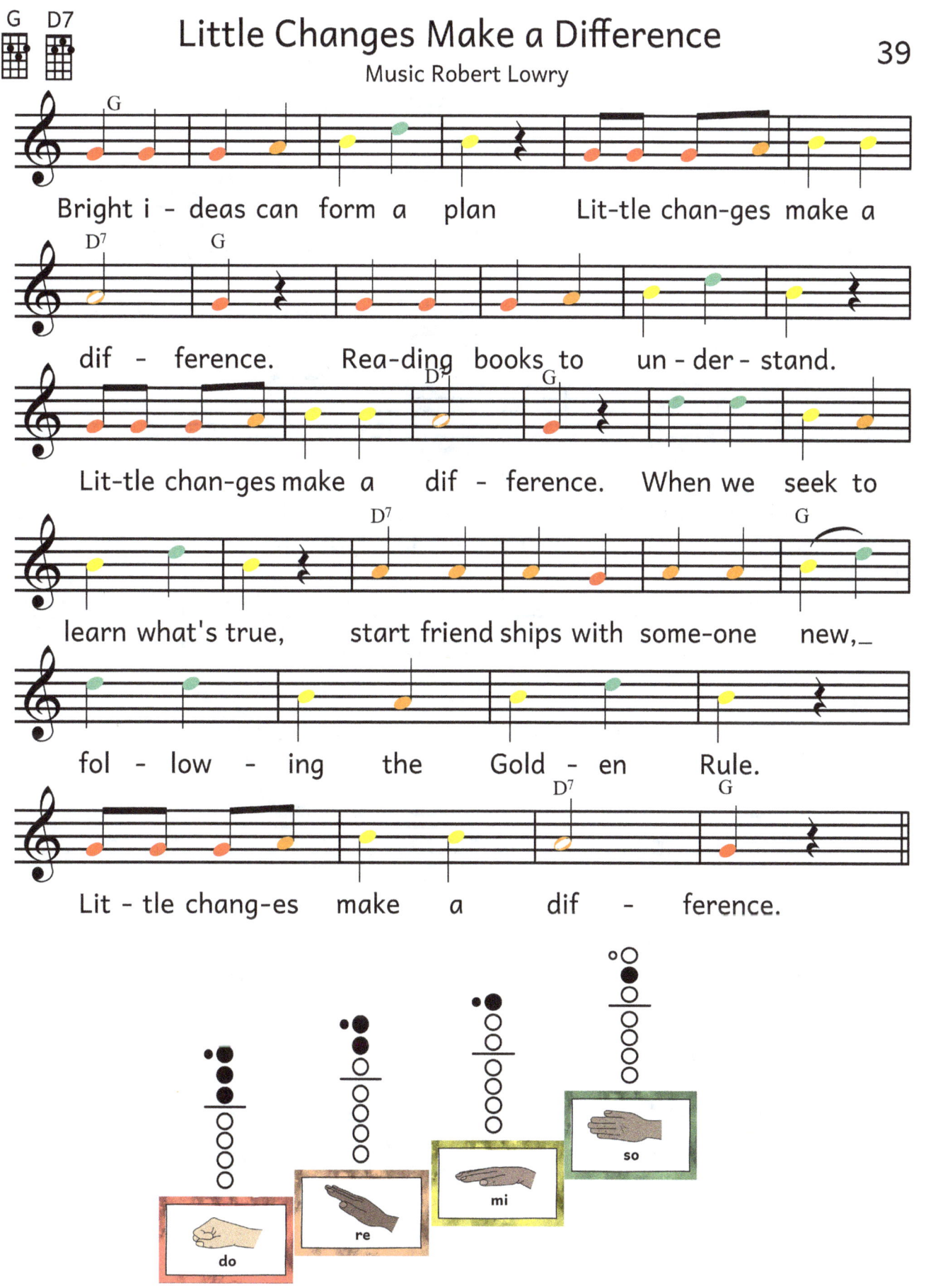

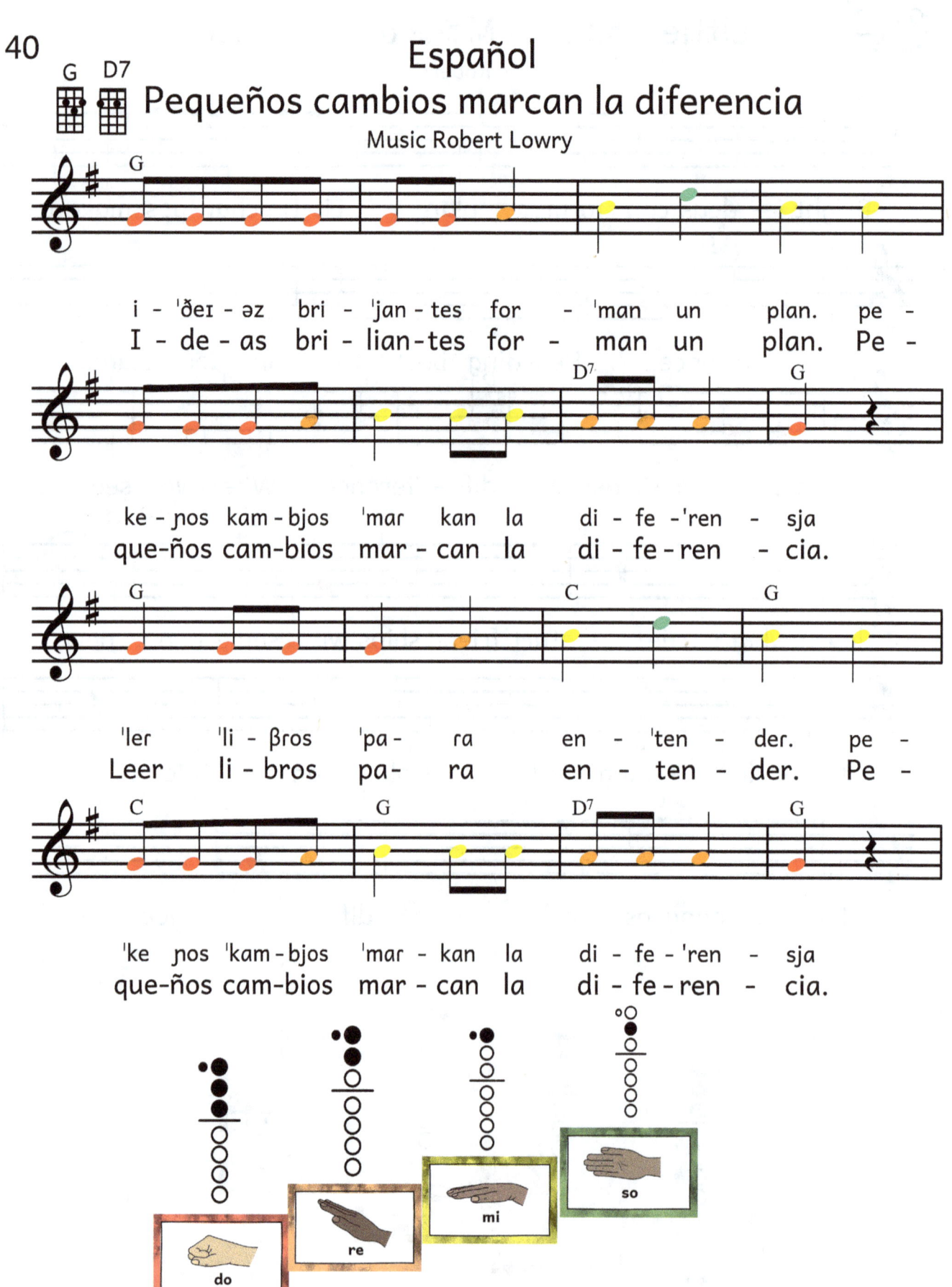

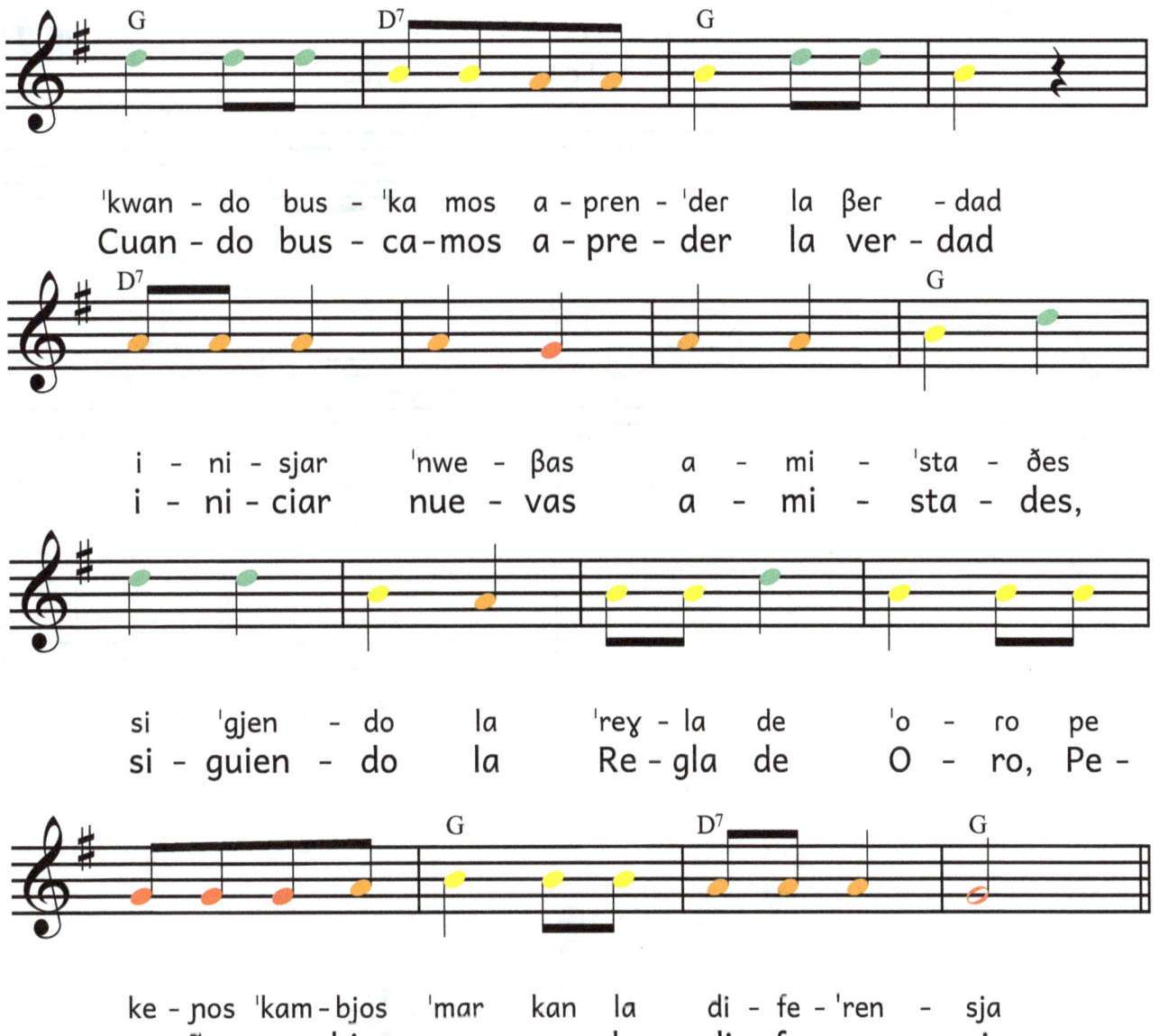

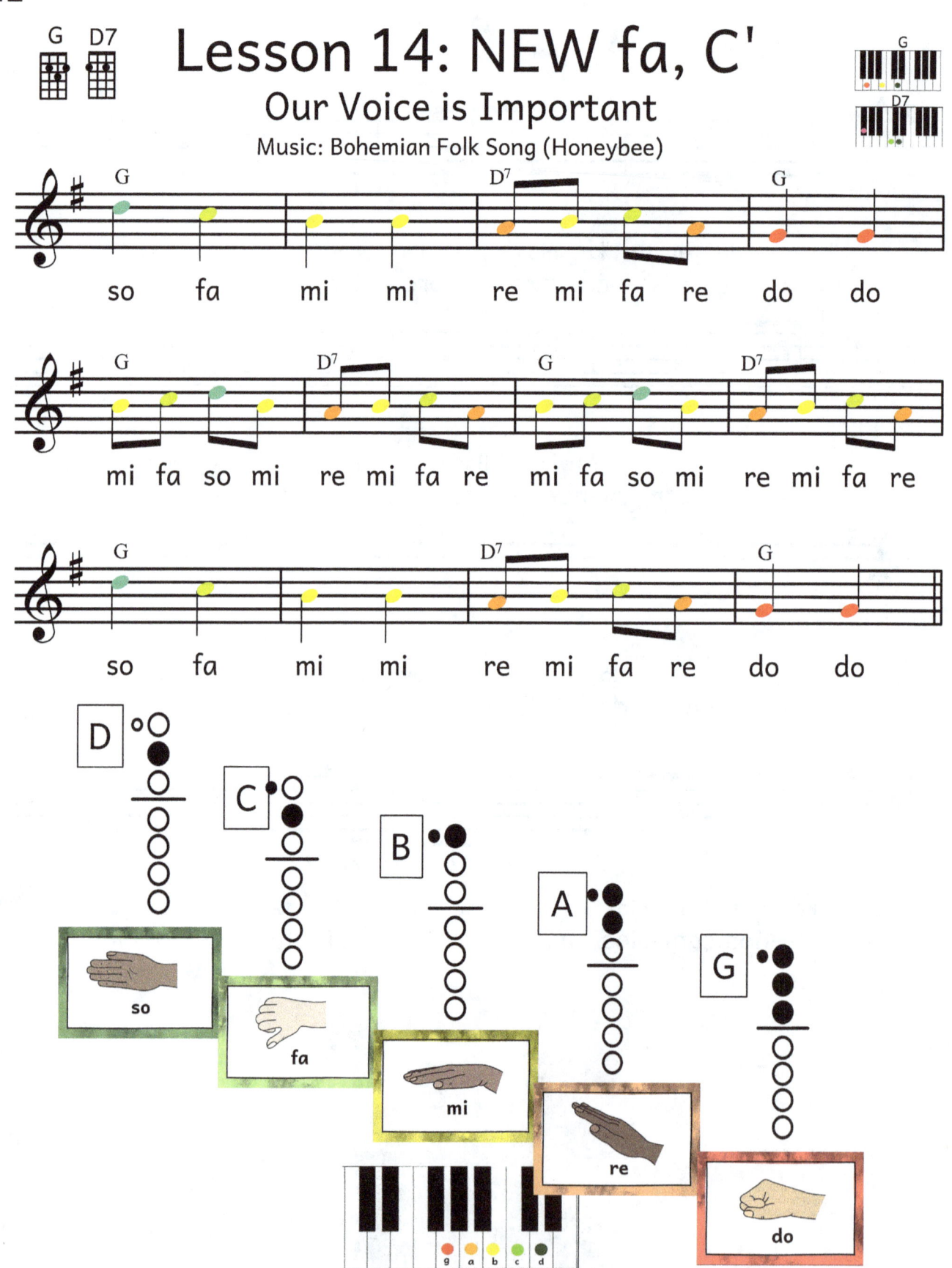

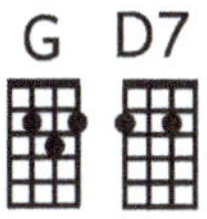

English
Our Voice is Important
Music: Bohemian Folk Song (Honeybee)

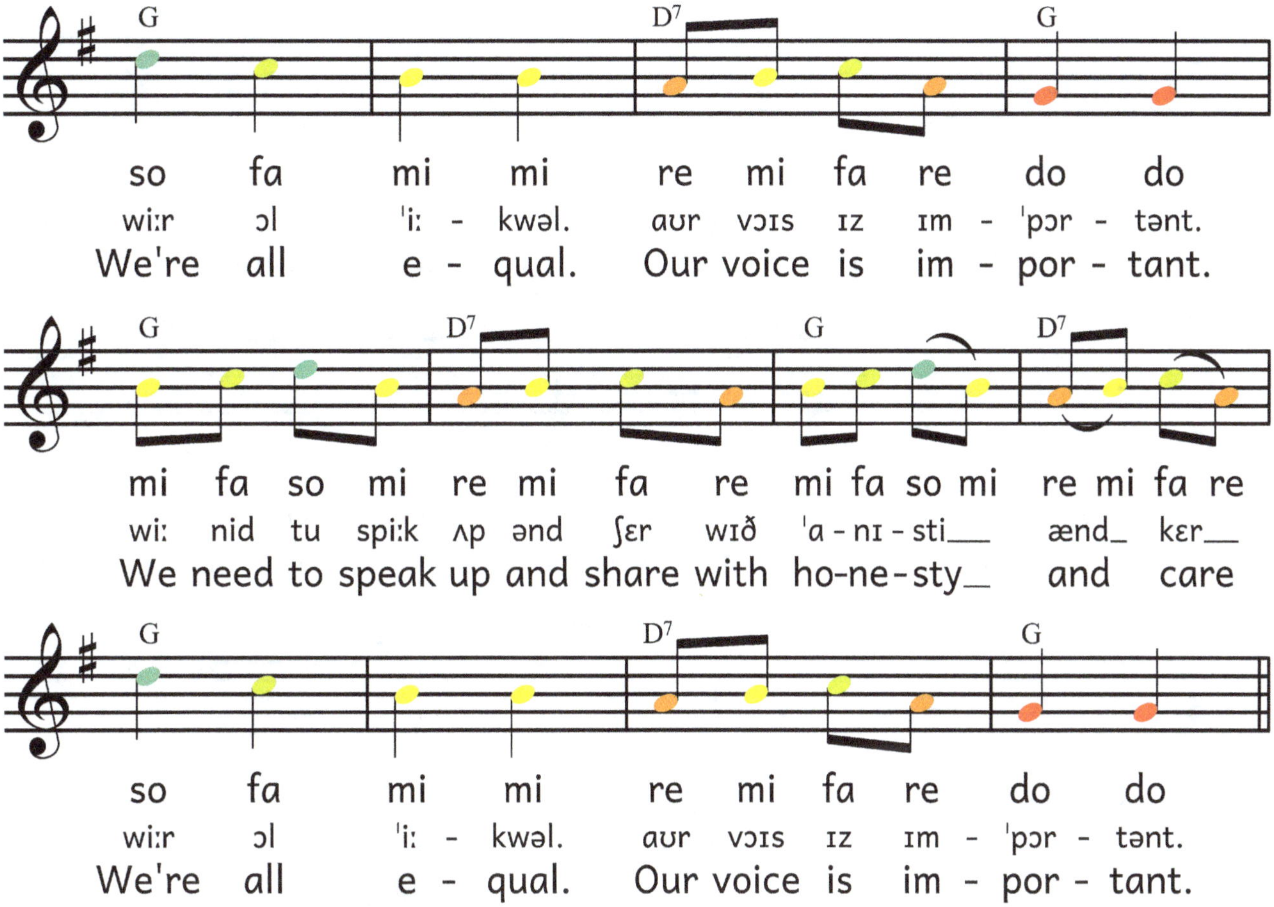

so fa mi mi re mi fa re do do
wiːr ɔl 'iː - kwəl. aʊr vɔɪs ɪz ɪm - 'pɔr - tənt.
We're all e - qual. Our voice is im - por - tant.

mi fa so mi re mi fa re mi fa so mi re mi fa re
wiː nid tu spiːk ʌp ənd ʃɛr wɪð 'a - nɪ - sti__ ænd__ kɛr__
We need to speak up and share with ho - ne - sty__ and care

so fa mi mi re mi fa re do do
wiːr ɔl 'iː - kwəl. aʊr vɔɪs ɪz ɪm - 'pɔr - tənt.
We're all e - qual. Our voice is im - por - tant.

Traditional lyrics:
Honeybee, buzzing busily,
Making honey from a flower
hour after busy hour.
Honeybee, see the honeybee.

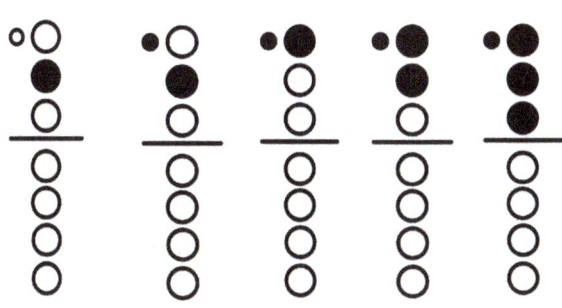

Copyright © 2024 Sarah Samuelson Studio

Español
Nuestra voz importa
Music: Bohemian Folk Song (Honeybee)

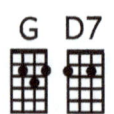

'to - dos 'so - mos i - 'gwa - les. 'nwes - tra 'βos im - 'por - ta
To-dos so-mos i - gua-les. Nue-stra voz im - por - ta.

ne - se - 'si - ta - mos a - 'blar i kom - par - 'tir kon o - ne - 'sti dað
Ne - ce - si - ta - mos ha-blar y com - par - tir con ho - ne - sti - dad.

'to - dos 'so - mos i - 'gwa - les. 'nwes - tra 'βos im - 'por - ta
To-dos so-mos i - gua-les. Nue-stra voz im - por - ta.

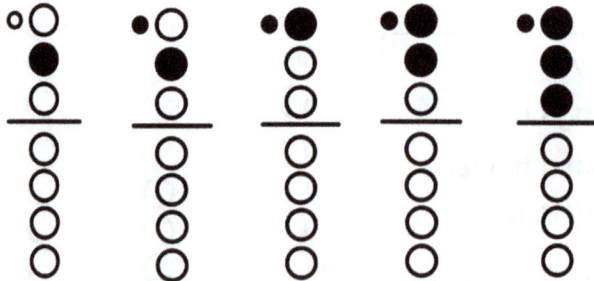

Copyright © 2024 Sarah Samuelson Studio

Lesson 15: New Tone fa
Stay Hopeful
Music: Sarah Samuelson

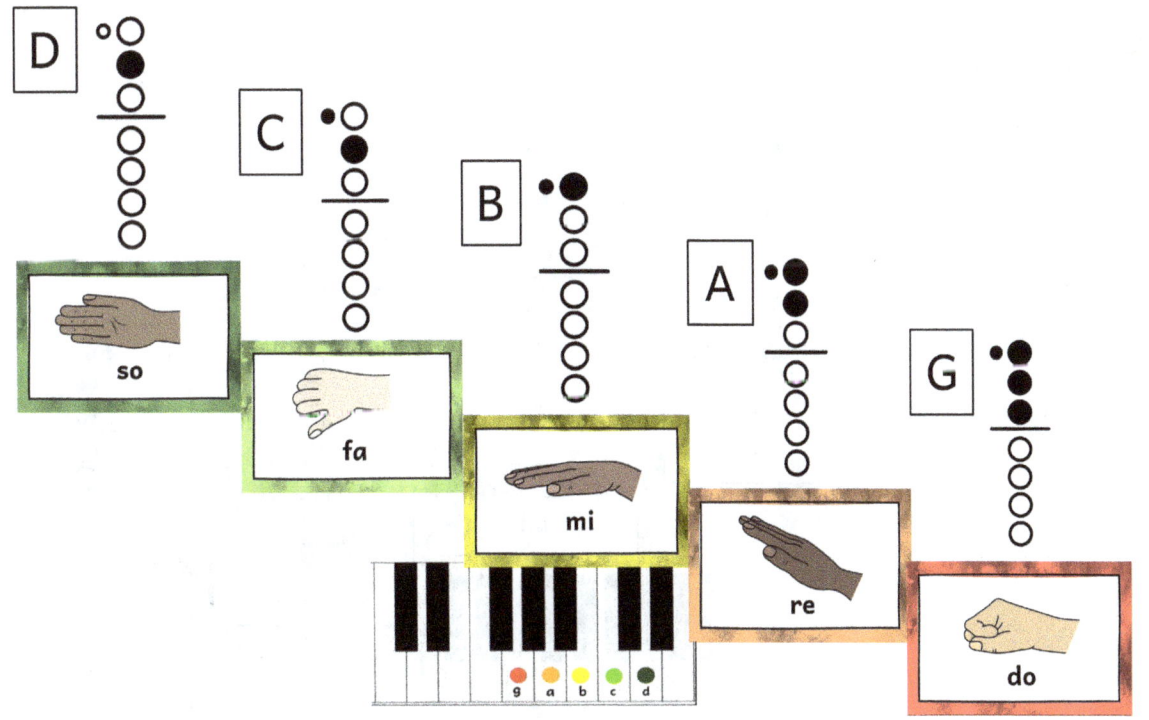

English
Stay Hopeful
Music: Sarah Samuelson

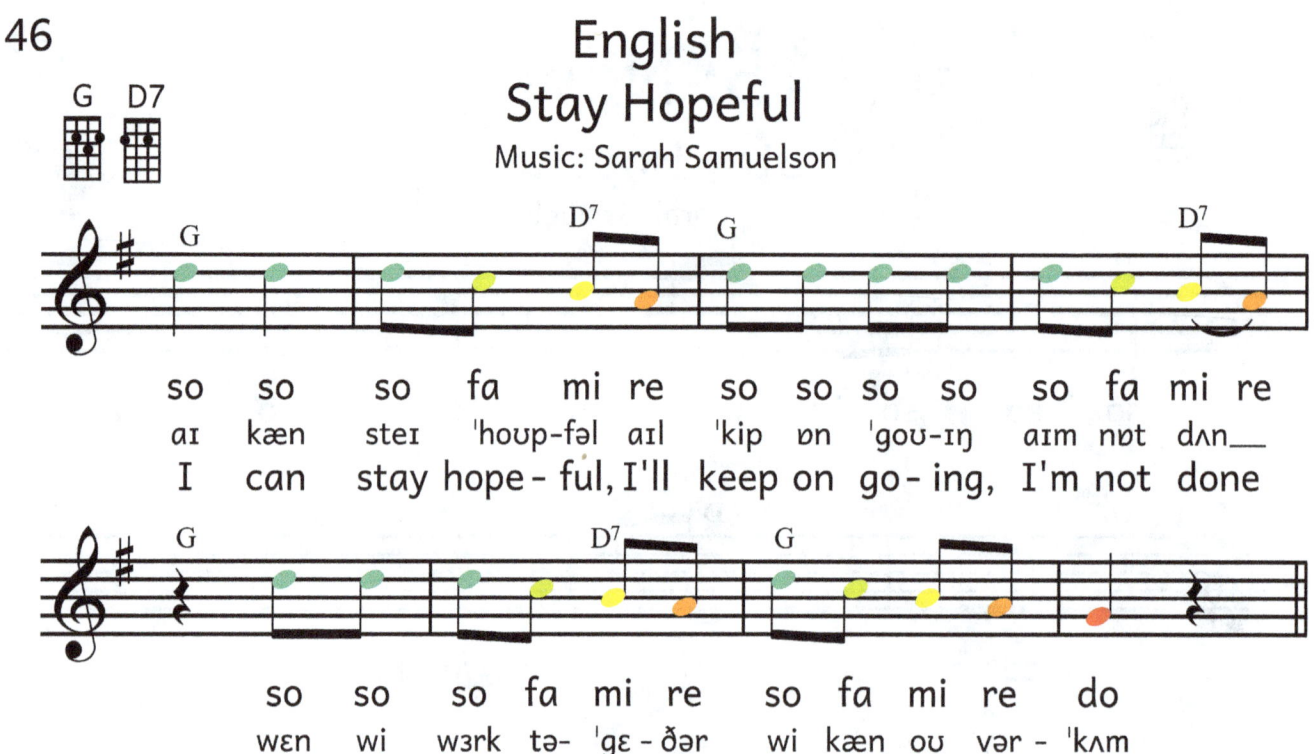

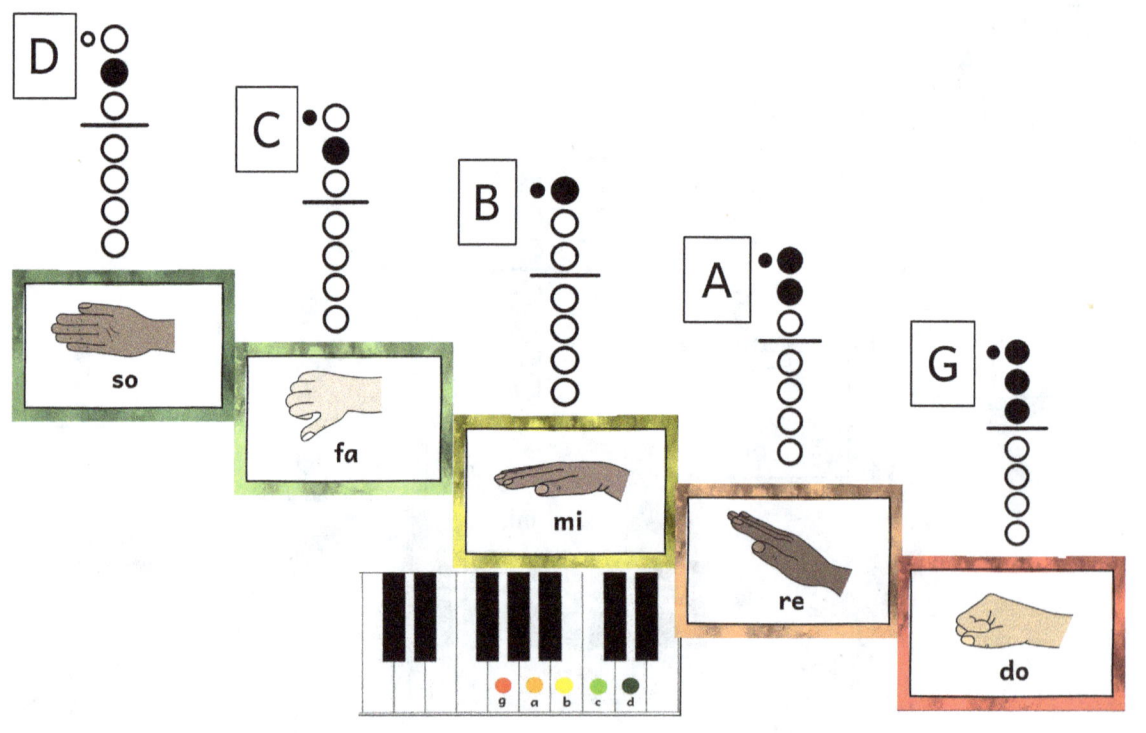

Copyright © 2024 Sarah Samuelson Studio

Español
Puedo tener esperanza
Music: Sarah Samuelson

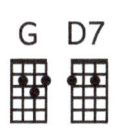

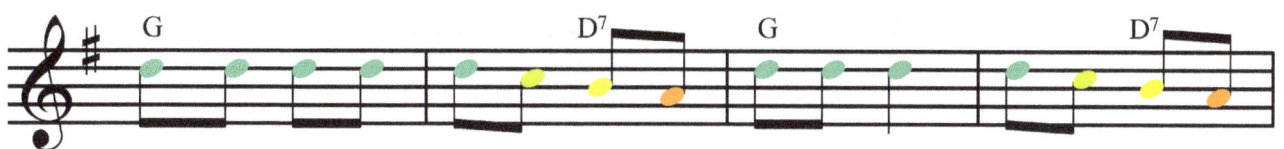

ˈpwe-do te-ˈner es-pe-ˈran-sa se-gi-ˈre a-ðe-ˈlan-te
Pue-do te-ner es-pe-ran-za; se-gui-ré a-de-lan-te

tra-βa-ˈxan-do ˈxun-tos, lo su pe - ˈra - mos
Tra-ba-jan-do jun-tos lo su pe - ra - mos.

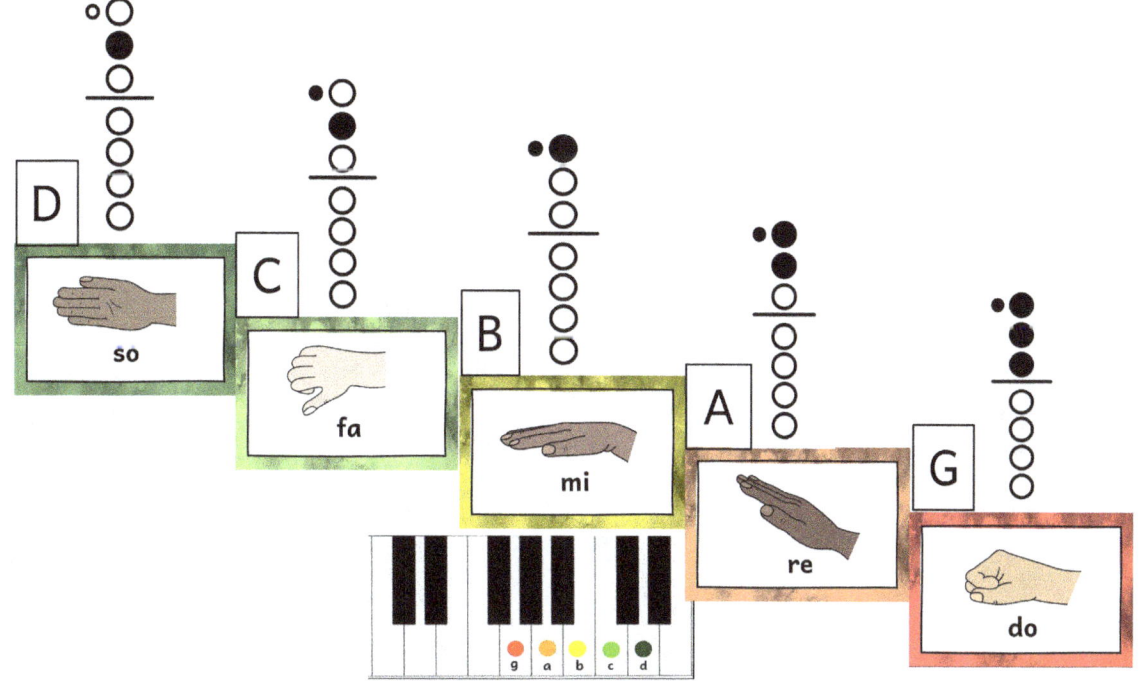

Copyright © 2024 Sarah Samuelson Studio

Lesson 16: NEW low so, D
Care For My Neighbor
Music: Germany (Mäh, Lämmchen, Mäh)

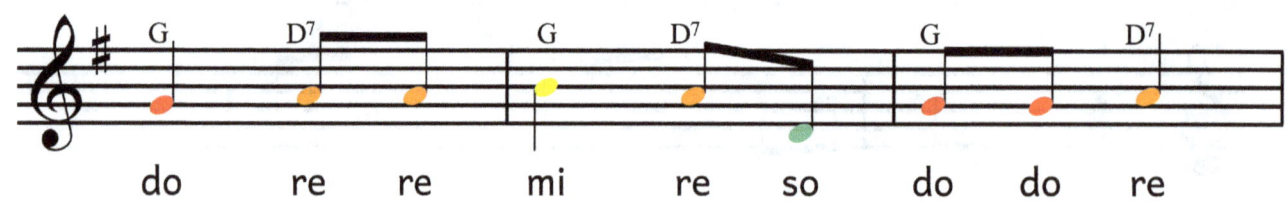
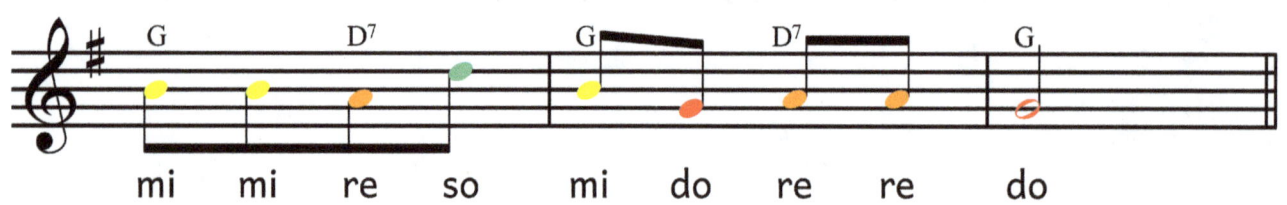
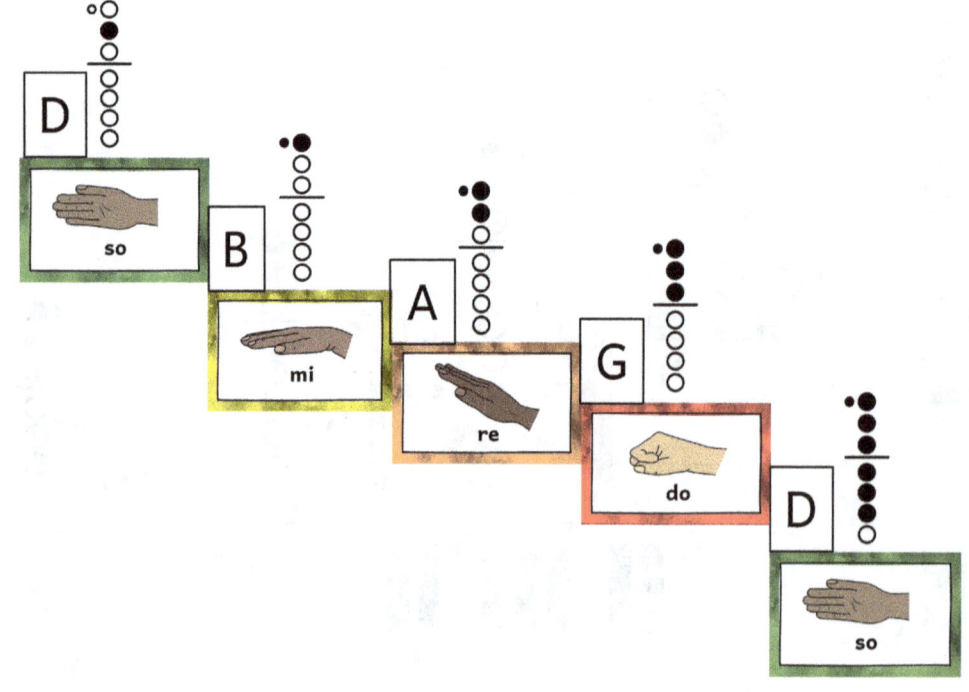

Copyright © 2024 Sarah Samuelson Studio

English
Care For My Neighbor
Music: Germany (Mäh, Lämmchen, Mäh)

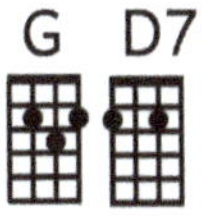

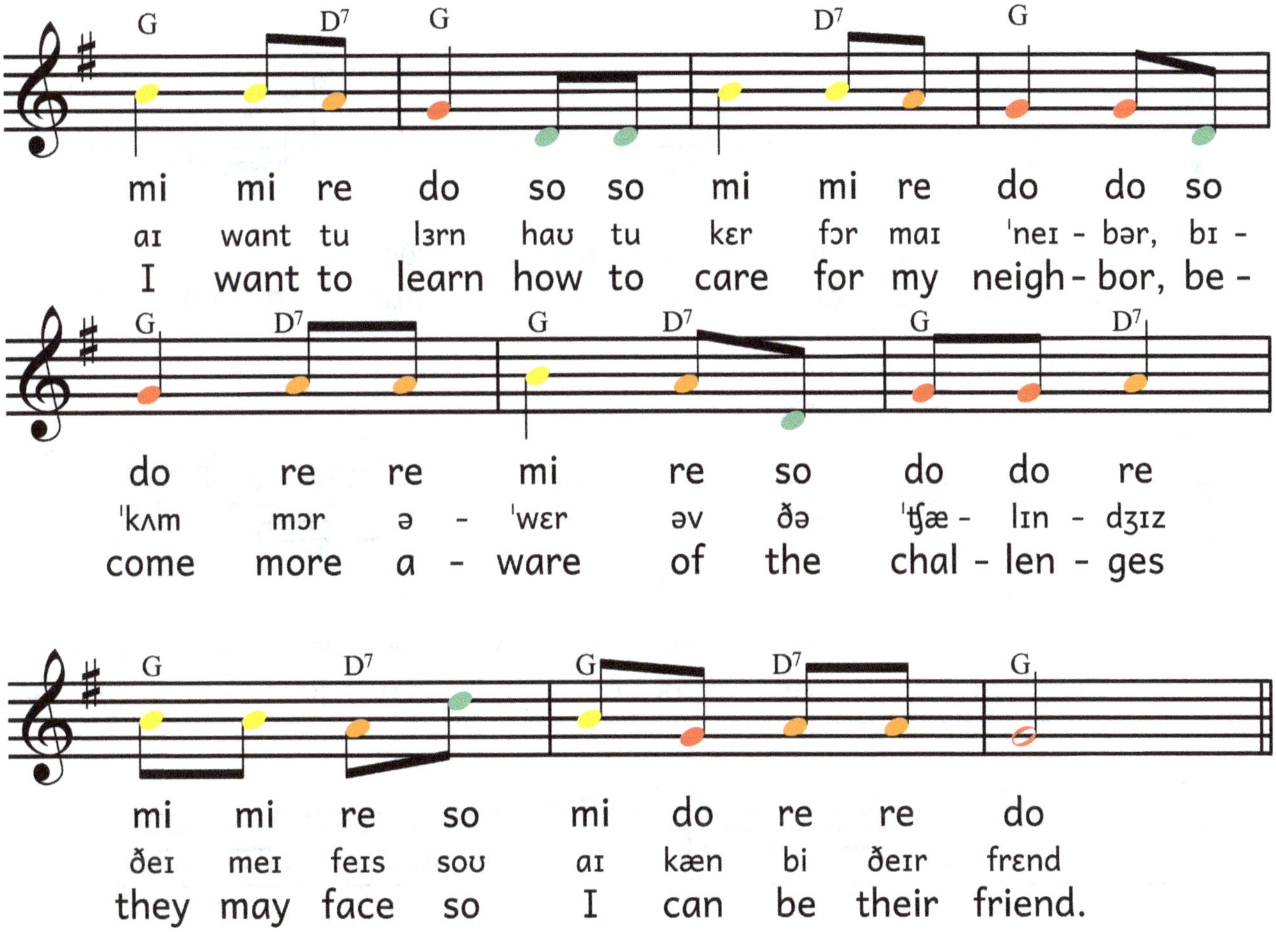

mi mi re do so so mi mi re do do so
aɪ wɑnt tu lɜrn haʊ tu kɛr fɔr maɪ ˈneɪ-bər, bɪ-
I want to learn how to care for my neigh-bor, be-

do re re mi re so do do re
ˈkʌm mɔr ə-ˈwɛr əv ðə ˈtʃæ-lɪn-dʒɪz
come more a-ware of the chal-len-ges

mi mi re so mi do re re do
ðeɪ meɪ feɪs soʊ aɪ kæn bi ðɛr frɛnd
they may face so I can be their friend.

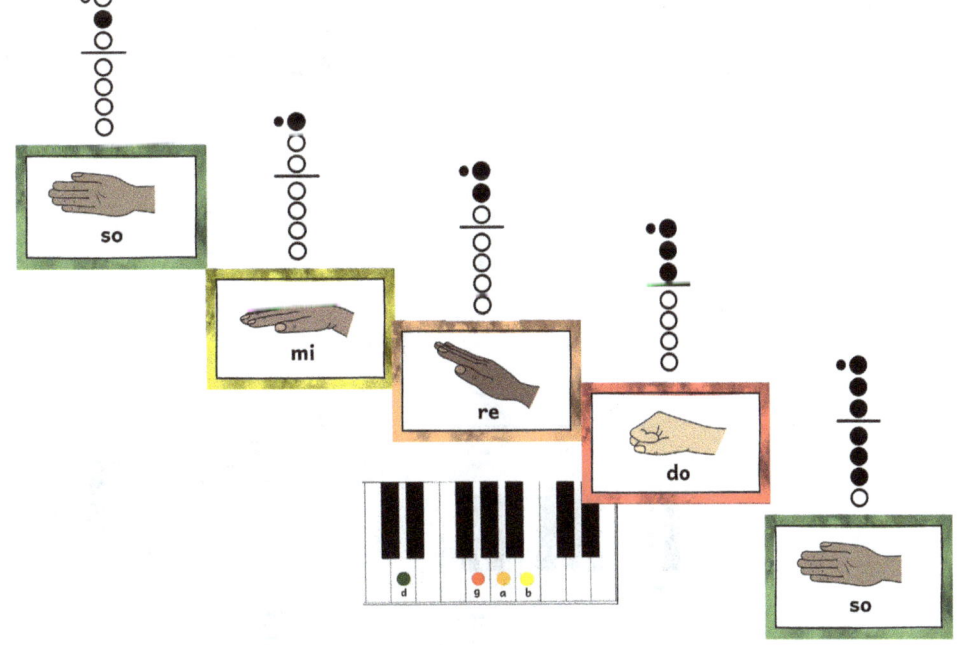

Copyright © 2024 Sarah Samuelson Studio

Español
Cuidar a mi Vecino

Music: Germany (Mäh, Lämmchen, Mäh)

ˈkje - ro a - pren - ˈder a kwi - ˈðar a mi be -
Quie - ro a - pren - der a cui - dar a mi ve -

ˈsi - no, ˈes - tar mas kon - ˈsjen - te de sus de - sa
ci - no, es - tar más con - scien - te de sus de - sa

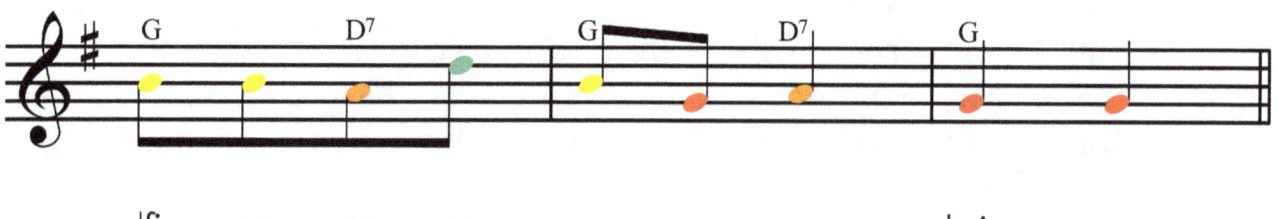

ˈfi - os pa - ra ser su a - ˈmi - go
fí - os pa - ra ser su a - mi - go.

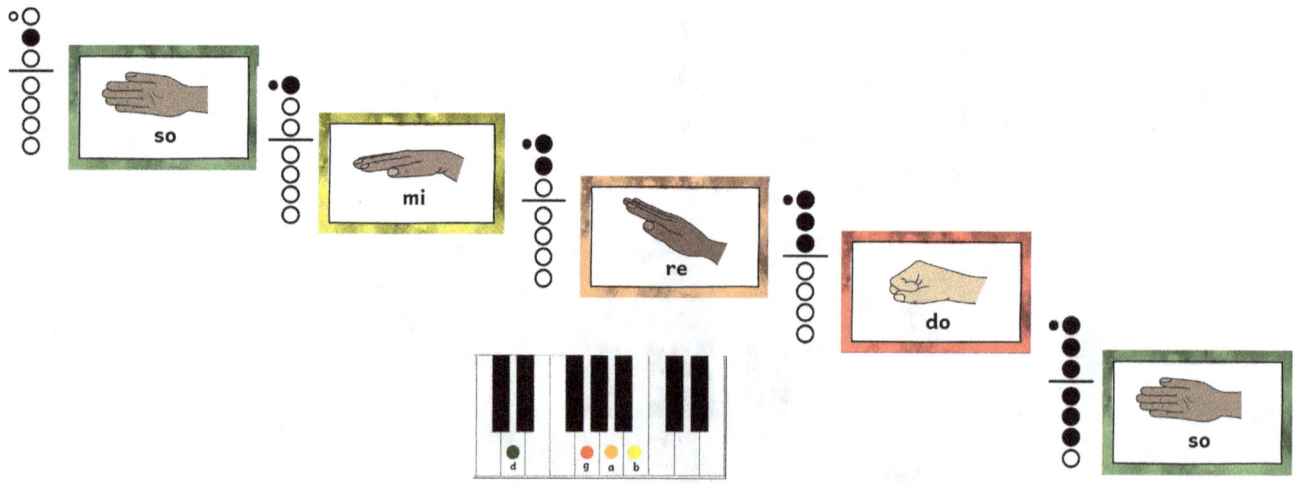

Copyright © 2024 Sarah Samuelson Studio

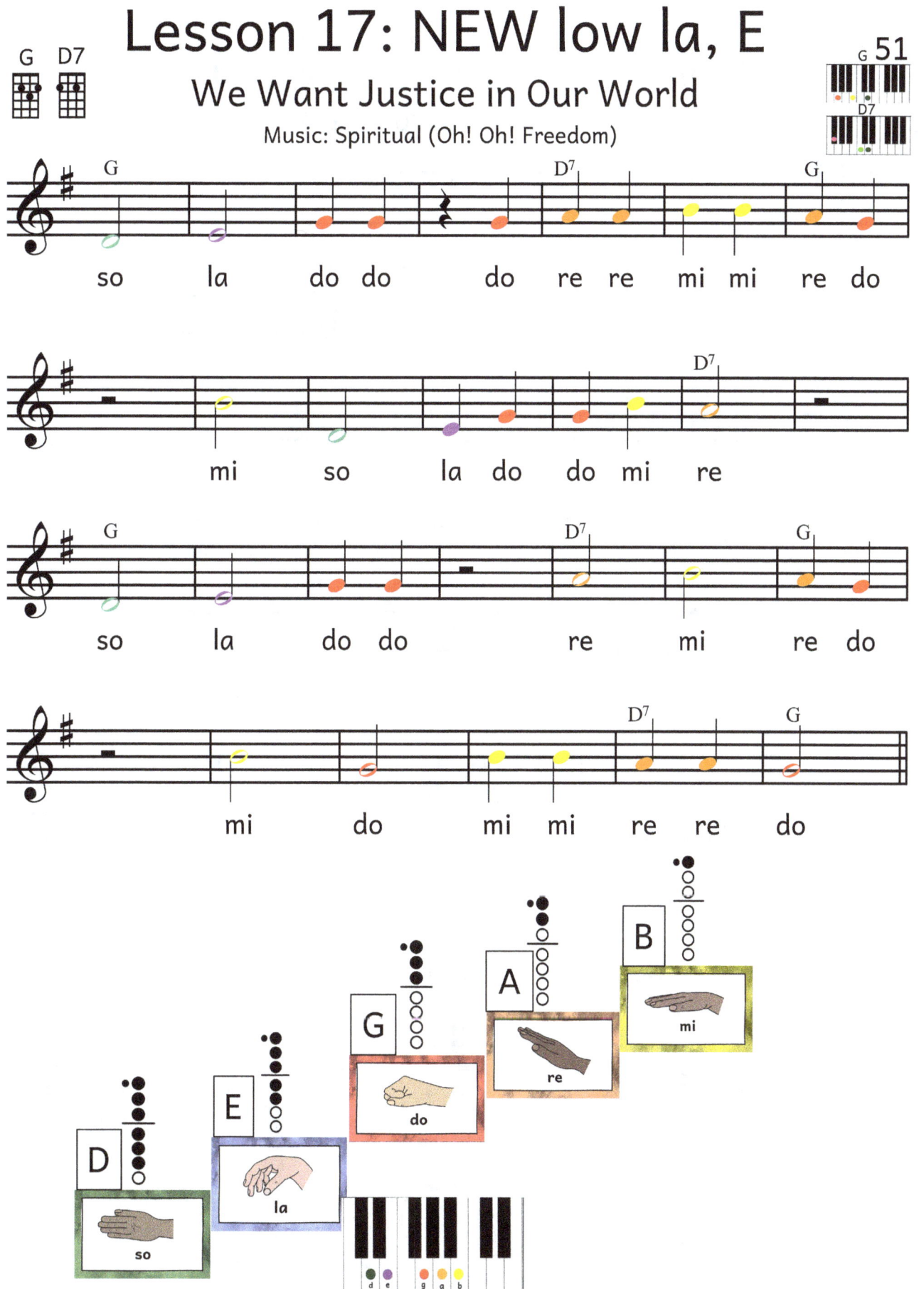

Español
Queremos Justicia en Nuestro Mundo
Music: Spiritual (Oh! Oh! Freedom)

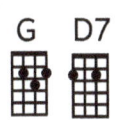

ke - 're - mos xu - 'stis - ja.　　kwi - 'ða-mos　'u-nos ðe
Que - re - mos ju - sti - cia.　　Cui - da-mos　u-nos de

'o - tros.　　ke - 're - mos xu - 'sti sja en 'nwes-tro 'mun - do
o - tros.　　Que - re - mos ju - sti-cia en nue-stro mun-do.

a - 'si ke hu - 'ɣa-mos bjen　　i 'mos-tra-mos kwi
A - si que ju - ga-mos bien　　y mo-stra-mos cui-

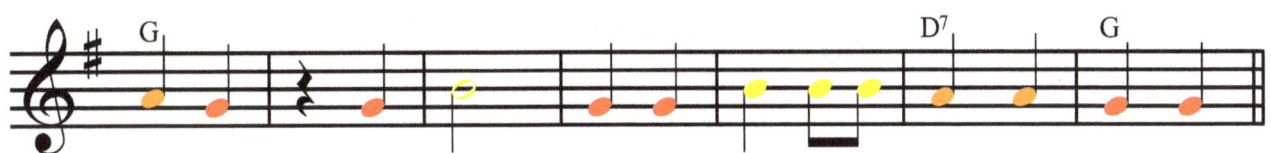

'ða - ðo.　　ke - 're - mos xu - 'stis ja en 'nwes-tro 'mun-do
da - do　　Que - re - mos ju - tis - ja en nue-stro mun-do

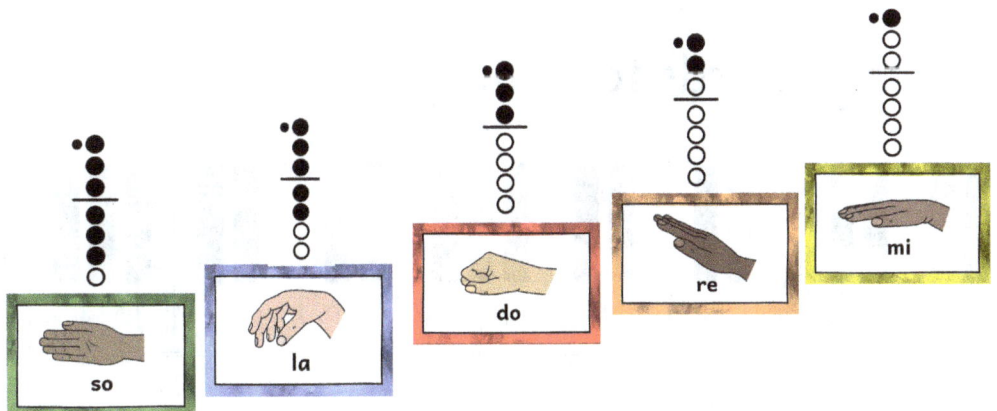

Copyright © 2024 Sarah Samuelson Studio

Lesson 18: new key of D, F#
Solfège D Major Scale

Notice the two sharps for the key of D

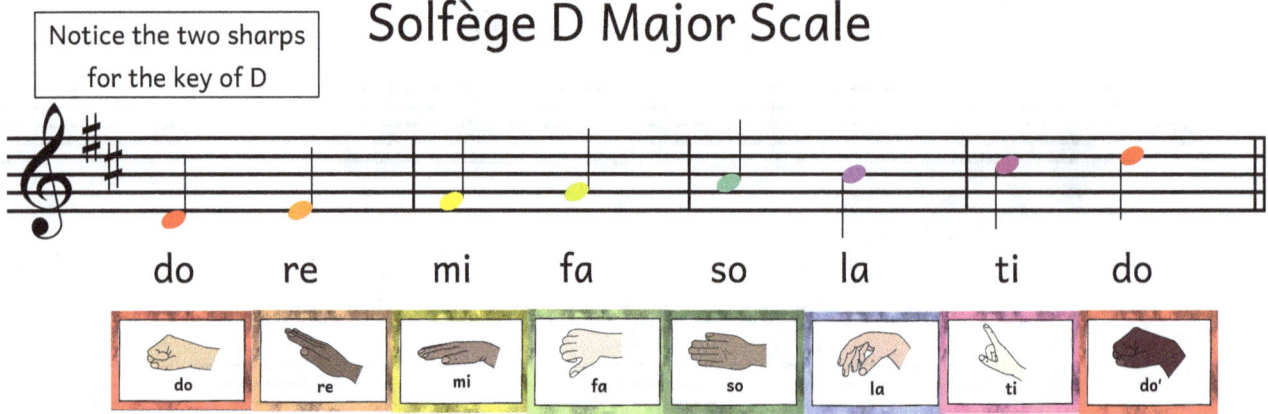

Solfège D Major Scale for Piano

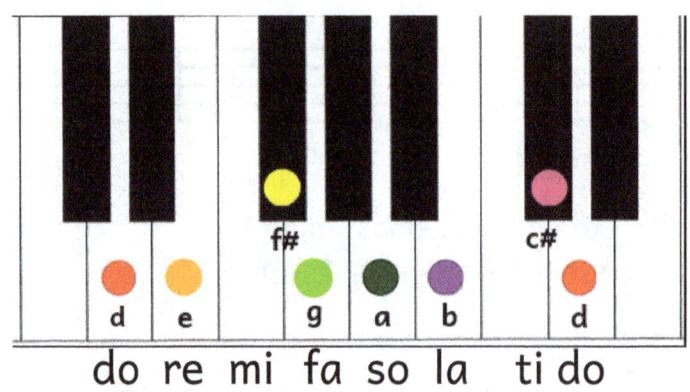

Chords for Piano - key of D

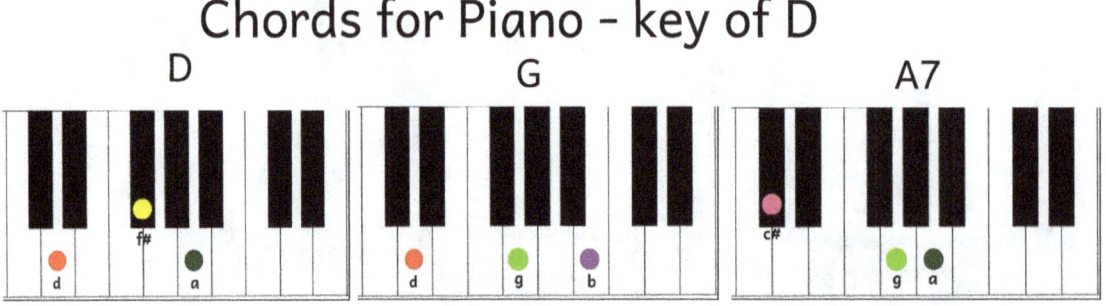

Copyright © 2024 Sarah Samuelson Studio

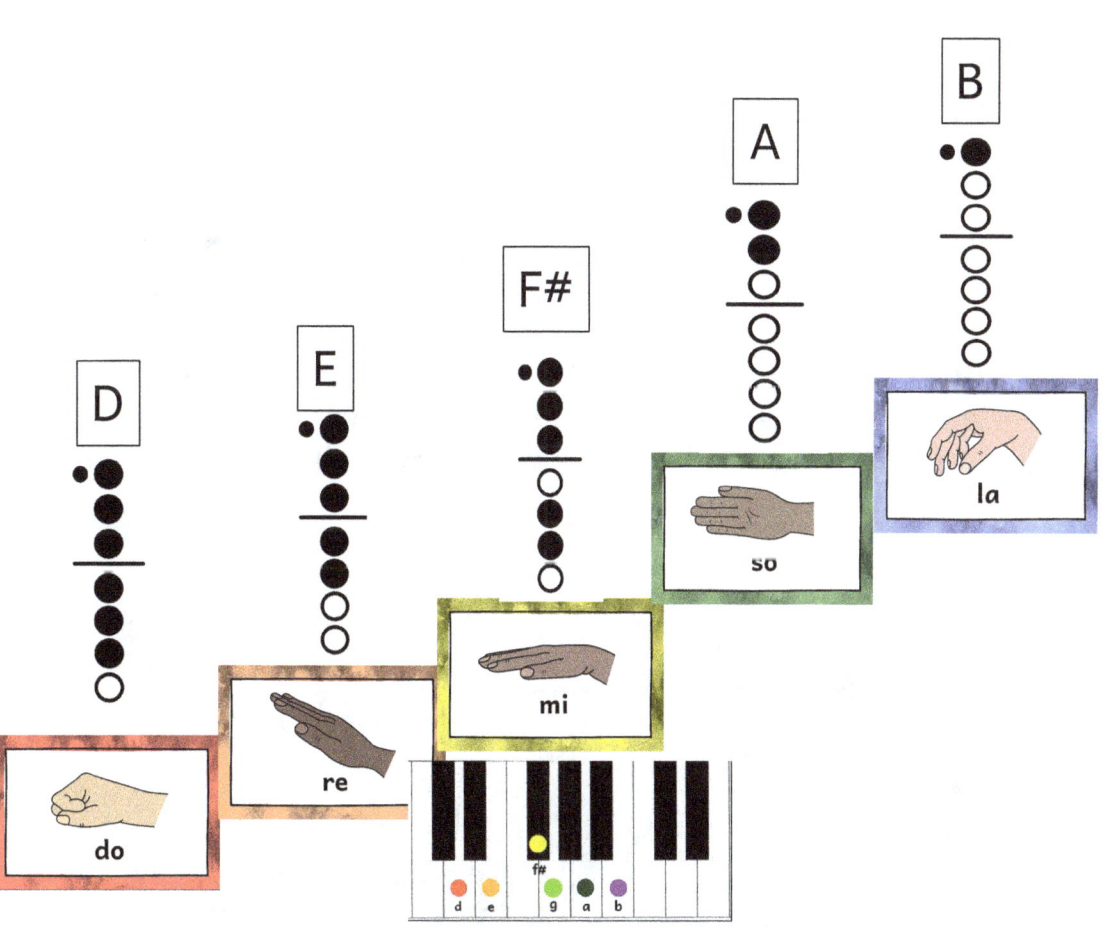

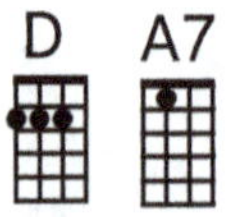

English
You are Important
Music: England (Here Comes a Bluebird)

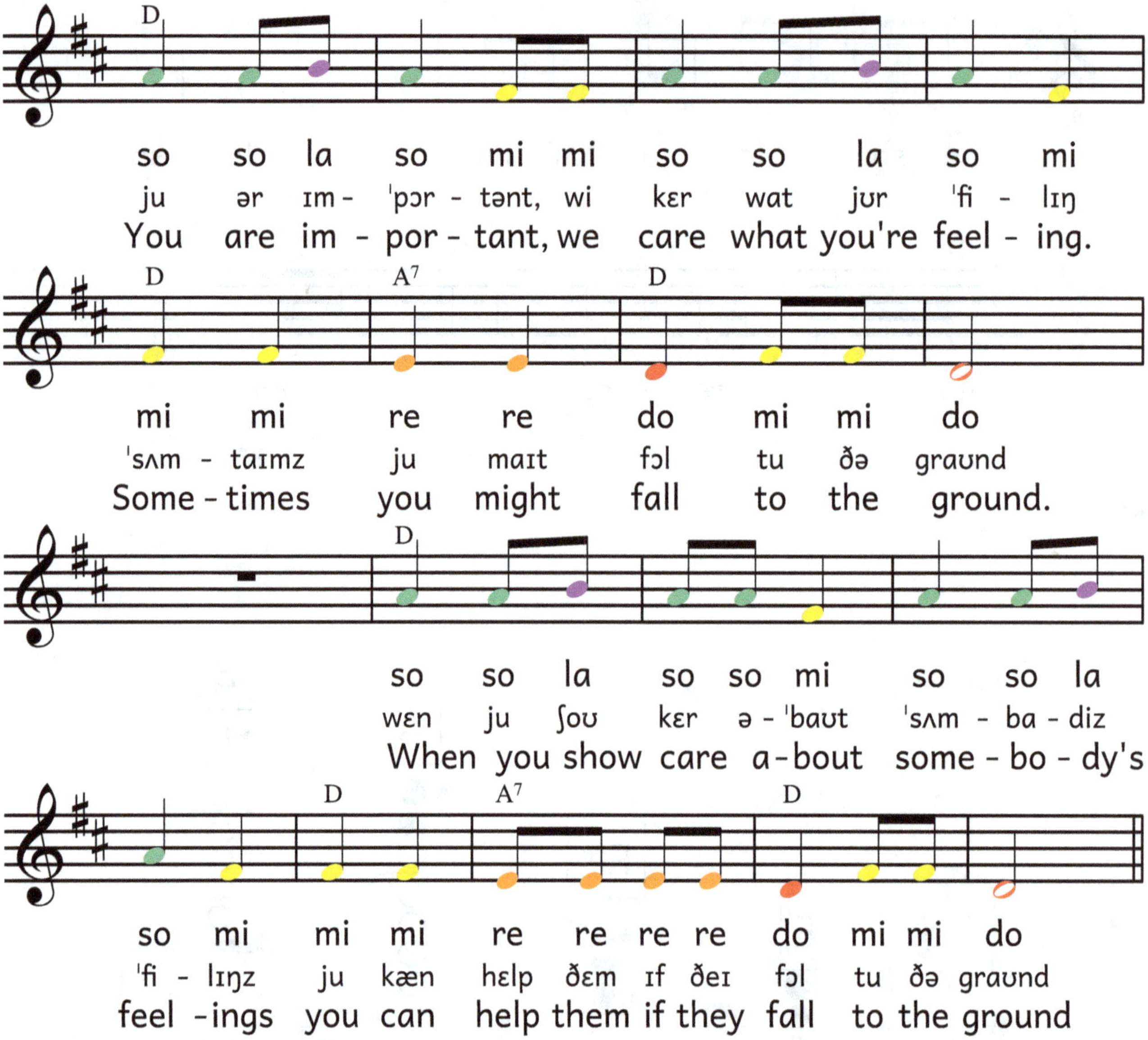

so so la so mi mi so so la so mi
ju ər ɪm-ˈpɔr-tənt, wi kɛr wat jʊr ˈfi-lɪŋ
You are im-por-tant, we care what you're feel-ing.

mi mi re re do mi mi do
ˈsʌm-taɪmz ju maɪt fɔl tu ðə graʊnd
Some-times you might fall to the ground.

so so la so so mi so so la
wɛn ju ʃoʊ kɛr ə-ˈbaʊt ˈsʌm-ba-diz
When you show care a-bout some-bo-dy's

so mi mi mi re re re re do mi mi do
ˈfi-lɪŋz ju kæn hɛlp ðɛm ɪf ðeɪ fɔl tu ðə graʊnd
feel-ings you can help them if they fall to the ground

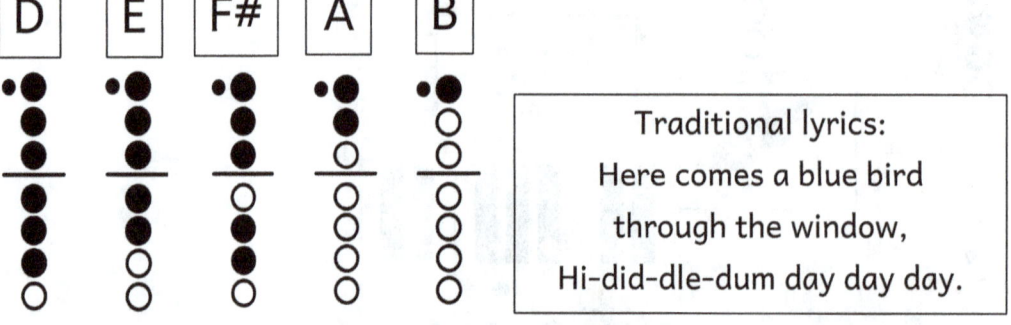

Traditional lyrics:
Here comes a blue bird
through the window,
Hi-did-dle-dum day day day.

Copyright © 2024 Sarah Samuelson Studio

Español
Eres importante
Music: Folk Song (Here Comes a Bluebird)

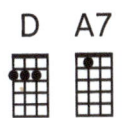

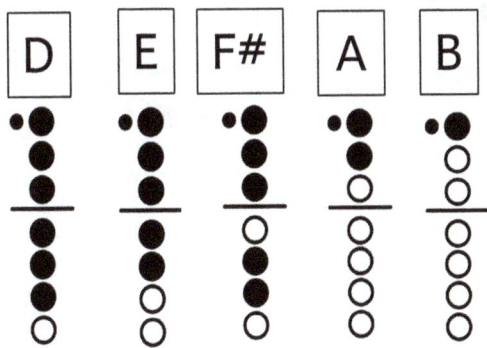

Lesson 19: key of D with F#
We Can Learn to Express Our Emotions
Music: Argentina (Los elefantes)

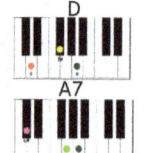

so so fa mi mi mi so so so fa mi mi so so la so fa mi

fa mi re fa fa fa mi re re fa fa mi

re re re so so so fa mi re mi re do

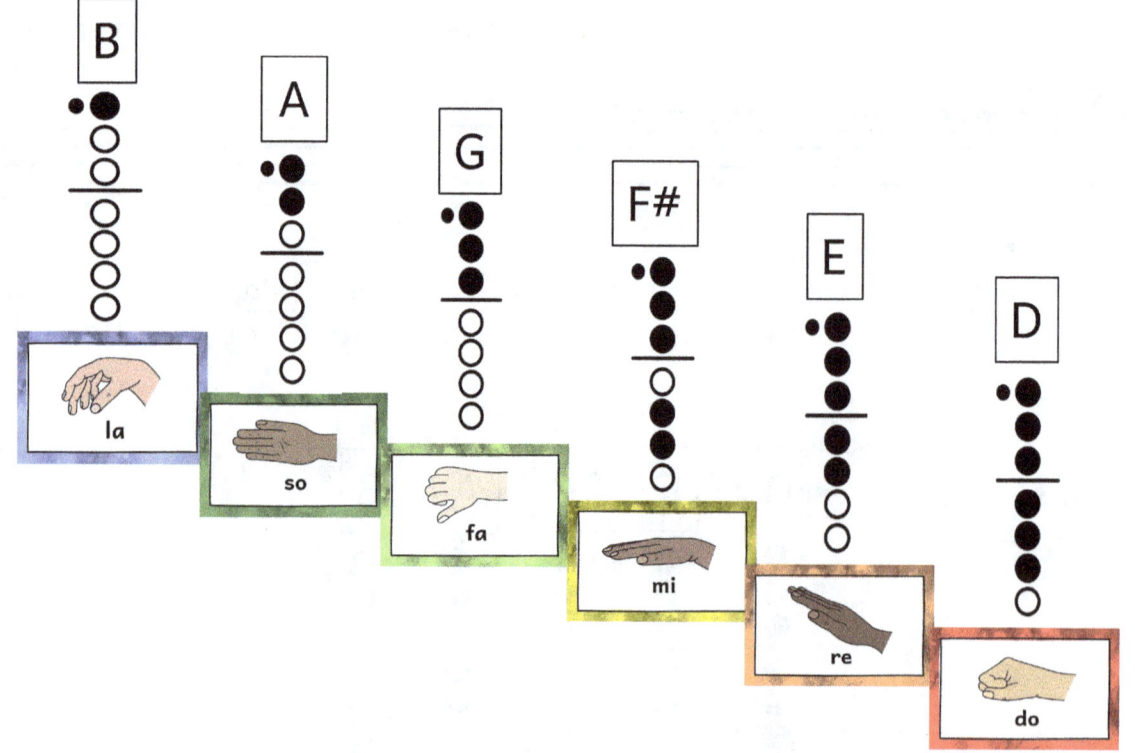

Copyright © 2024 Sarah Samuelson Studio

English
We Can Learn to Express Our Emotions
Music: Argentina (Los elefantes)

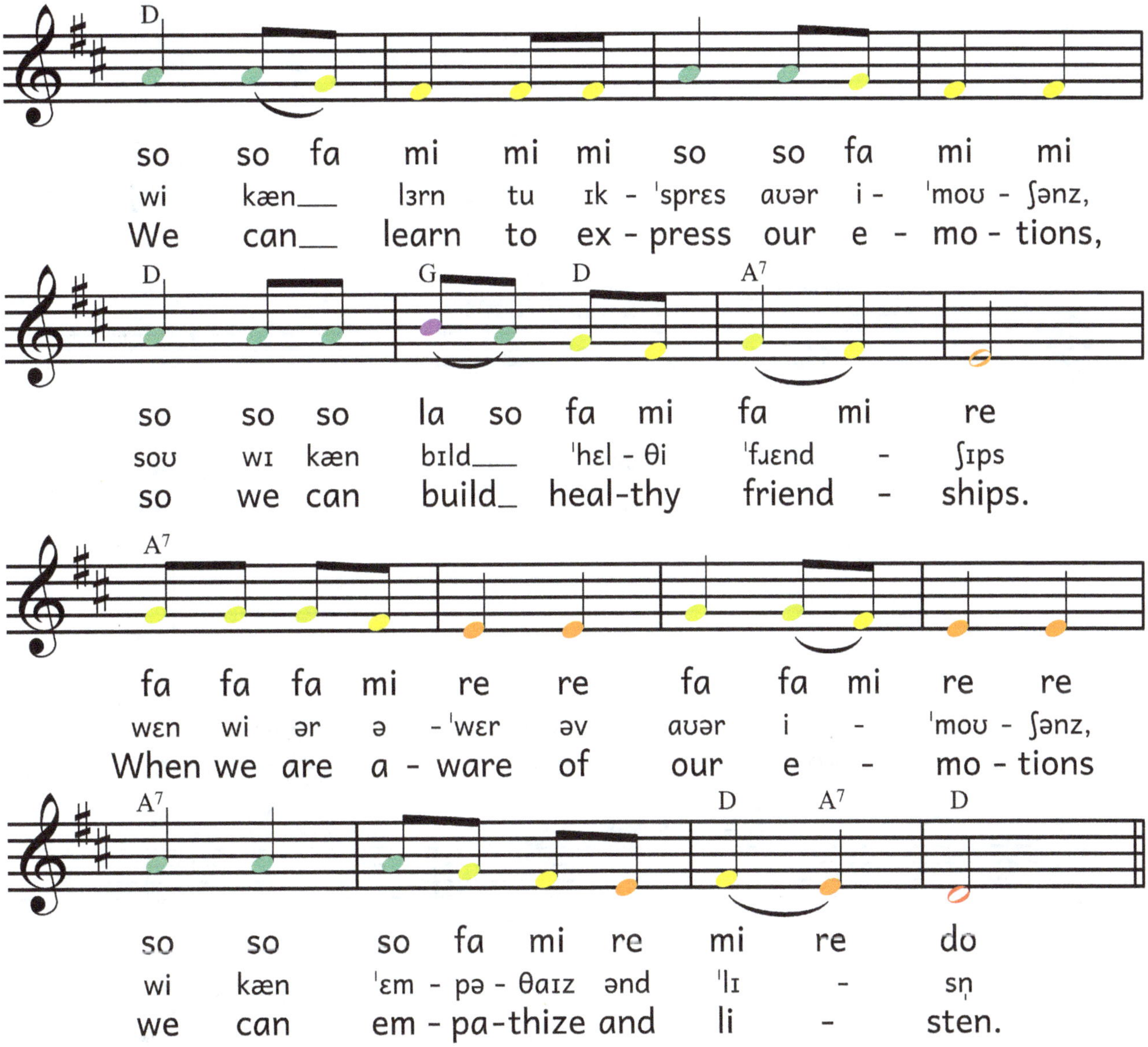

so so fa mi mi mi so so fa mi mi
wi kæn___ lɜrn tu ɪk-ˈsprɛs aʊər i-ˈmoʊ-ʃənz,
We can___ learn to ex-press our e-mo-tions,

so so so la so fa mi fa mi re
soʊ wi kæn bɪld___ ˈhɛl-θi ˈfɹɛnd-ʃɪps
so we can build___ heal-thy friend-ships.

fa fa fa mi re re fa fa mi re re
wɛn wi ər ə-ˈwɛr əv aʊər i-ˈmoʊ-ʃənz,
When we are a-ware of our e-mo-tions

so so so fa mi re mi re do
wi kæn ˈɛm-pə-θaɪz ənd ˈlɪ-sn̩
we can em-pa-thize and li-sten.

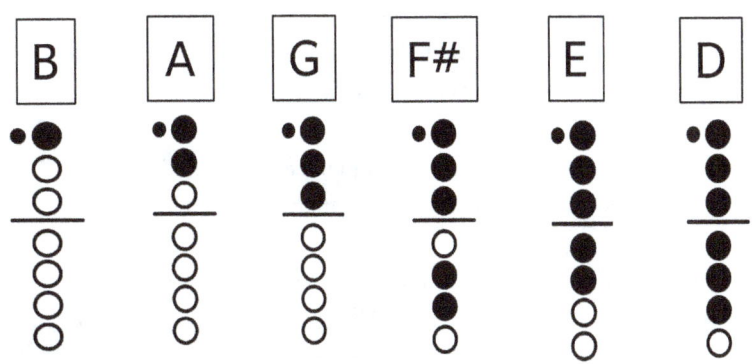

Copyright © 2024 Sarah Samuelson Studio

Español
Aprendemos a expresar emociones
Music: Argentina (Los elefantes)

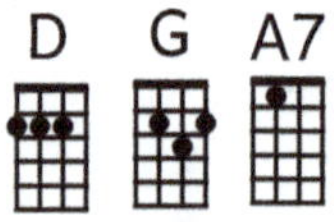

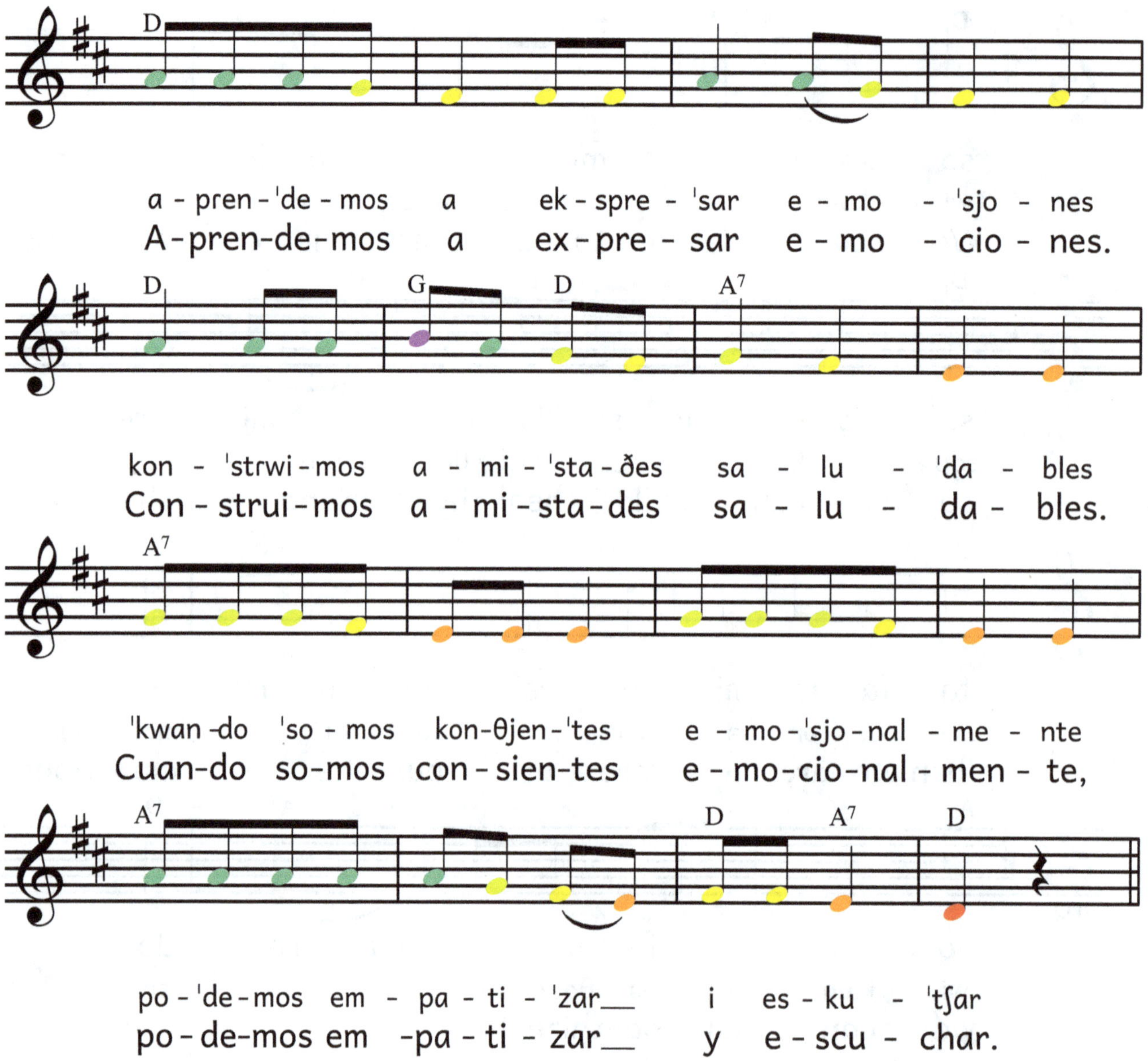

a - pren - 'de - mos   a   ek - spre - 'sar   e - mo - 'sjo - nes
A - pren - de - mos   a   ex - pre - sar   e - mo - cio - nes.

kon - 'strwi - mos   a - mi - 'sta - ðes   sa - lu - 'da - bles
Con - strui - mos   a - mi - sta - des   sa - lu - da - bles.

'kwan - do   'so - mos   kon - θjen - 'tes   e - mo - 'sjo - nal - me - nte
Cuan - do   so - mos   con - sien - tes   e - mo - cio - nal - men - te,

po - 'de - mos   em - pa - ti - 'zar__   i   es - ku - 'tʃar
po - de - mos   em - pa - ti - zar__   y   e - scu - char.

> Traditional Argentinian Song: Los Elefantes
> un e le 'fã te se βa lan se_a βa   so βre la te la ðe_u na ra ɲa
> Un elefante se balance aba   sobre la tela de_una_araña
>
> ko mo βe i a ke re si sti a fwe a ʝa ma ra_o tro_e le fã nte
> Como veîa, que resistía, fué a llamarra_otro_elefante.
>
> One elephant was balancing on a spider web
> How he saw that it resisted weight he went to call another elephant.

Copyright © 2024 Sarah Samuelson Studio

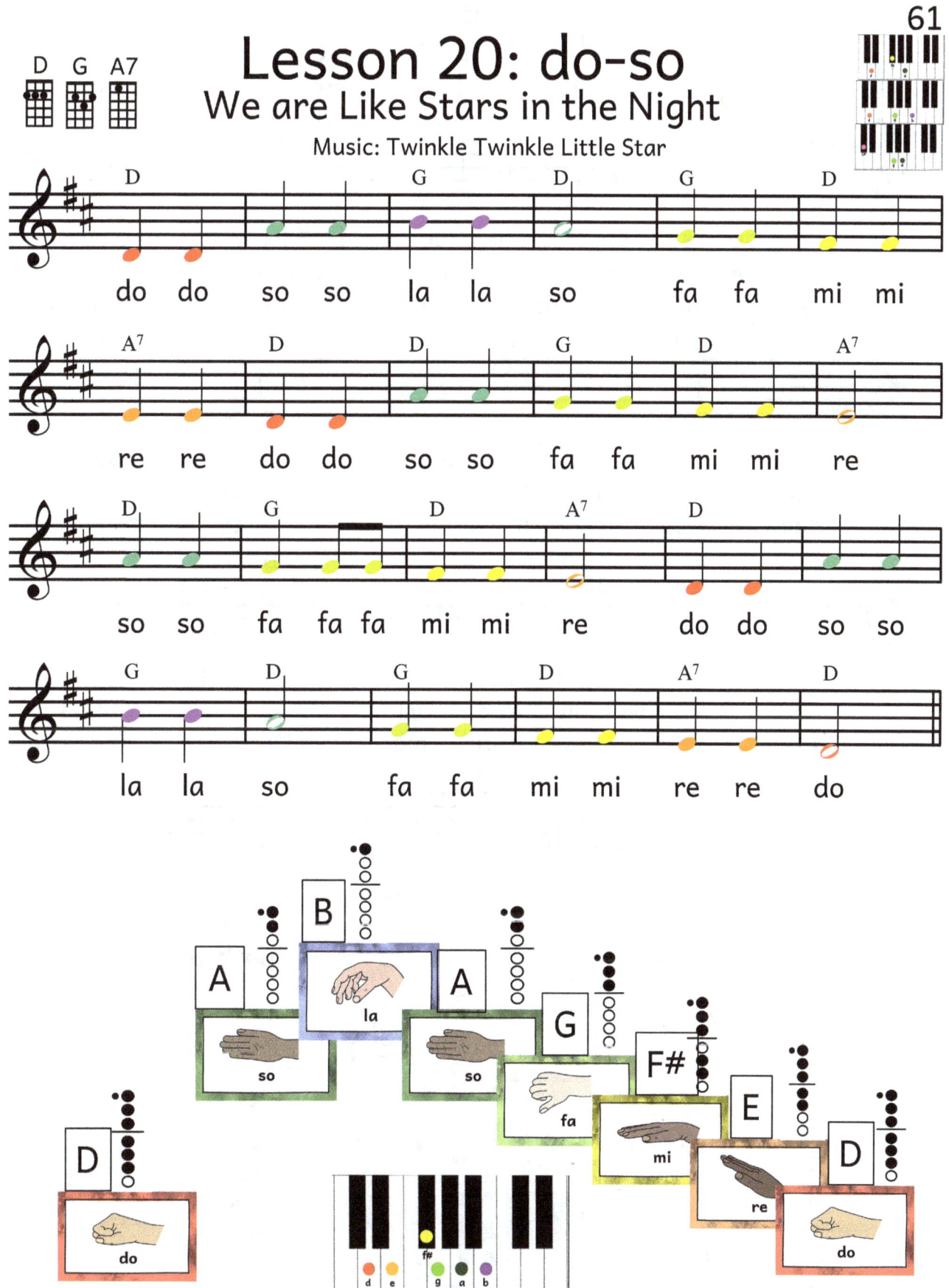

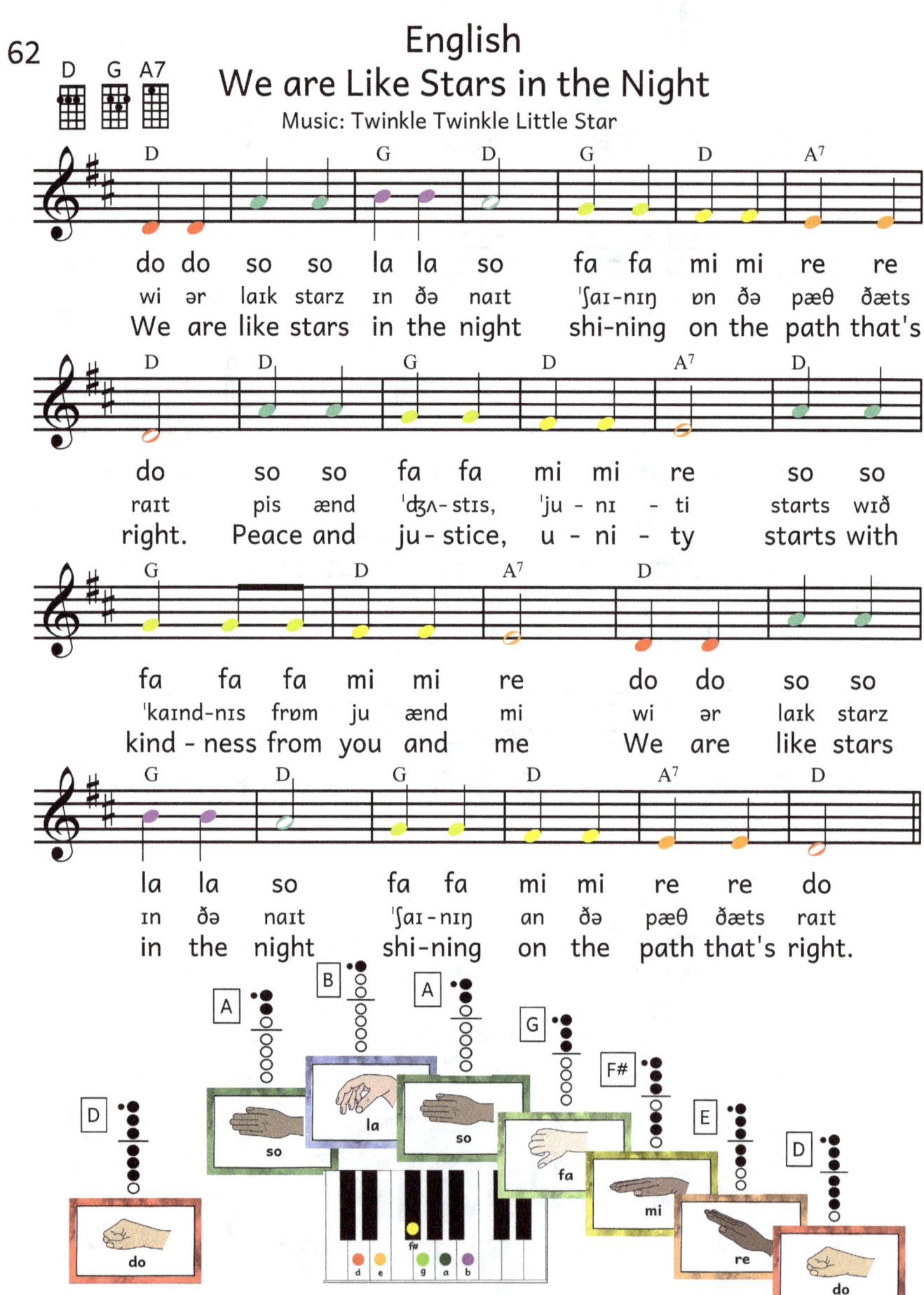

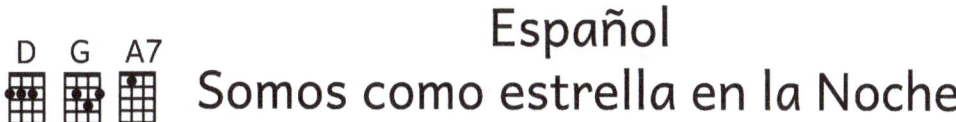
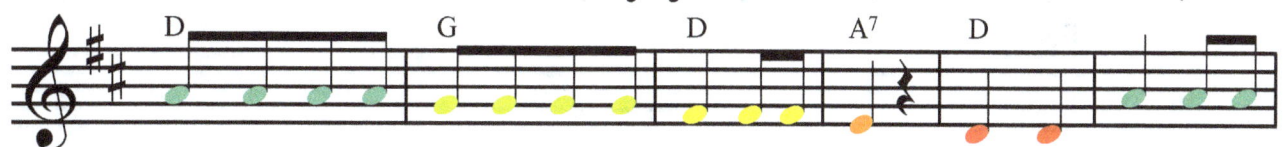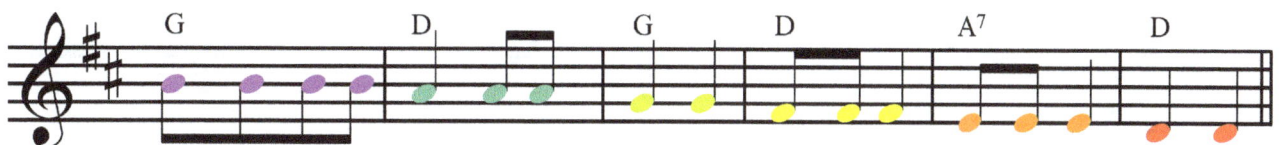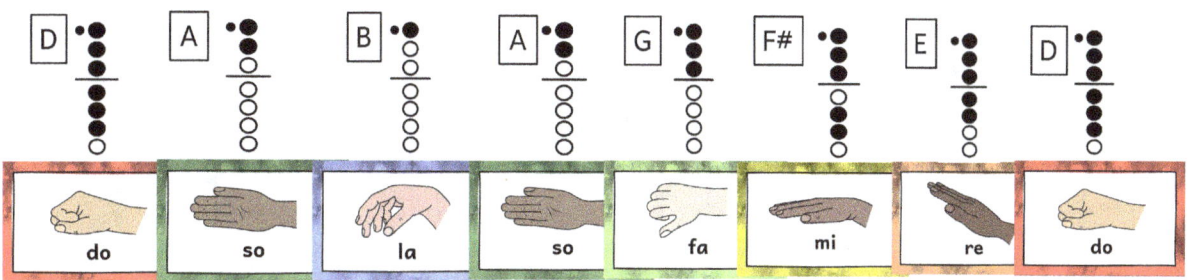

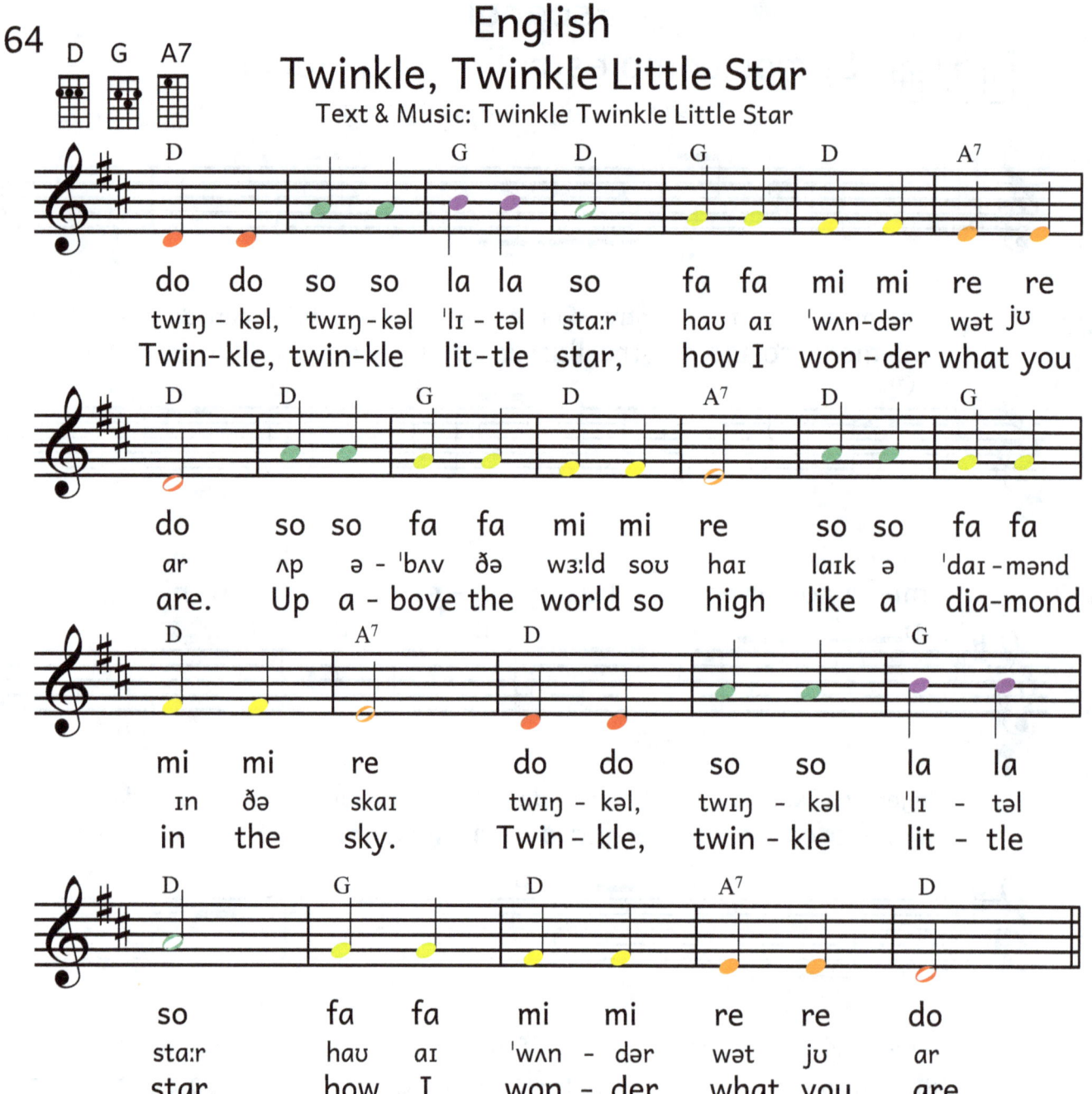

Español
Estrellita Donde Estas?

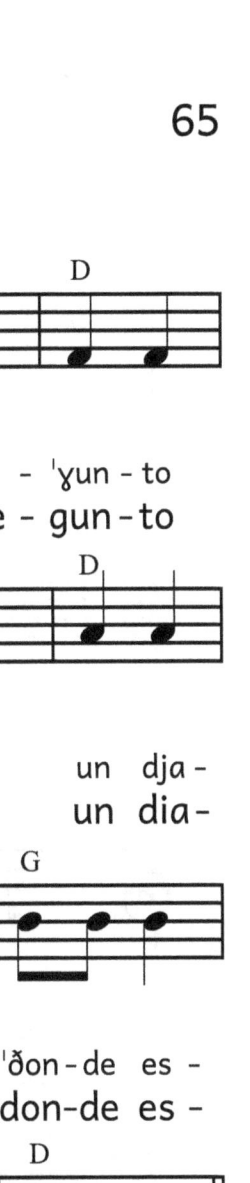

> Translation of Spanish
> Little star, where are you?
> I wonder what you are.
> In the sky and in the sea
> A real diamond
> Little star, where are you?
> I wonder what you are.

Copyright © 2024 Sarah Samuelson Studio

Français
Ah! vous dirai-je, Maman

Translation of French:
Oh! Shall I tell you, Mommy
What is bothering me?
Daddy wants me to reason
like a grown-up person,
Me, I say that sweets
Are worth more than reasoning.

Copyright © 2024 Sarah Samuelson Studio

Lesson 21: so-la
We All Have a Super Power
Music: Mexico (Chocolate molinillo)

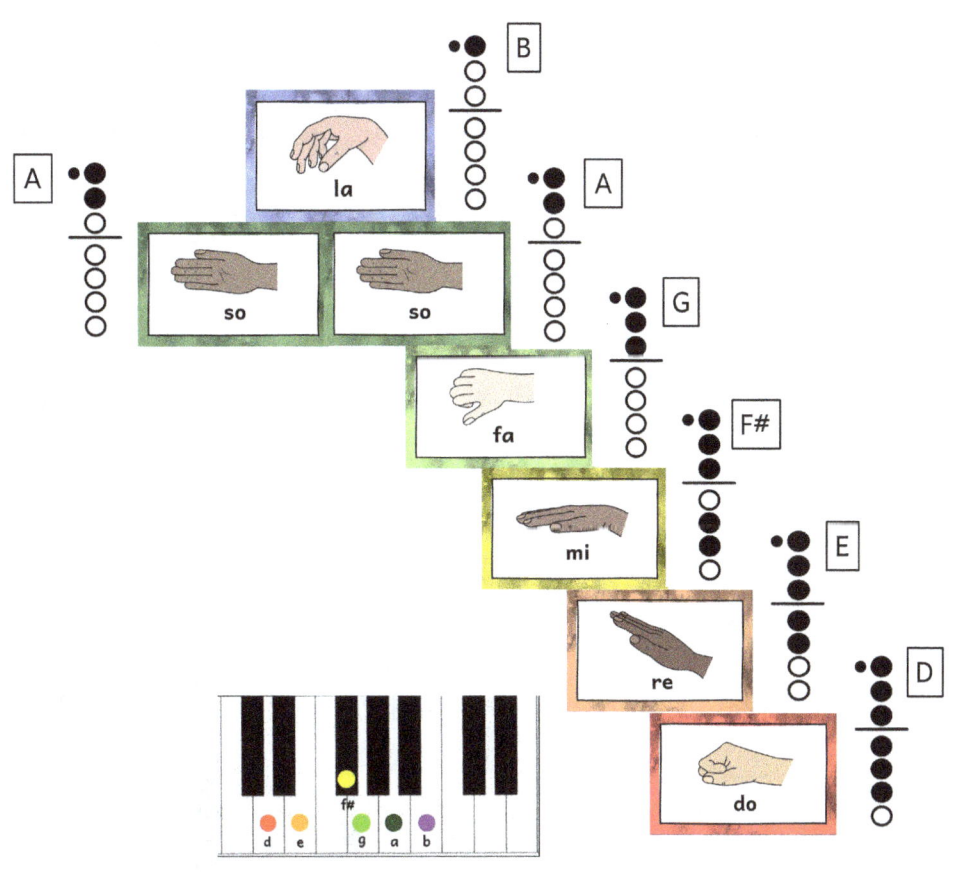

Copyright © 2024 Sarah Samuelson Studio

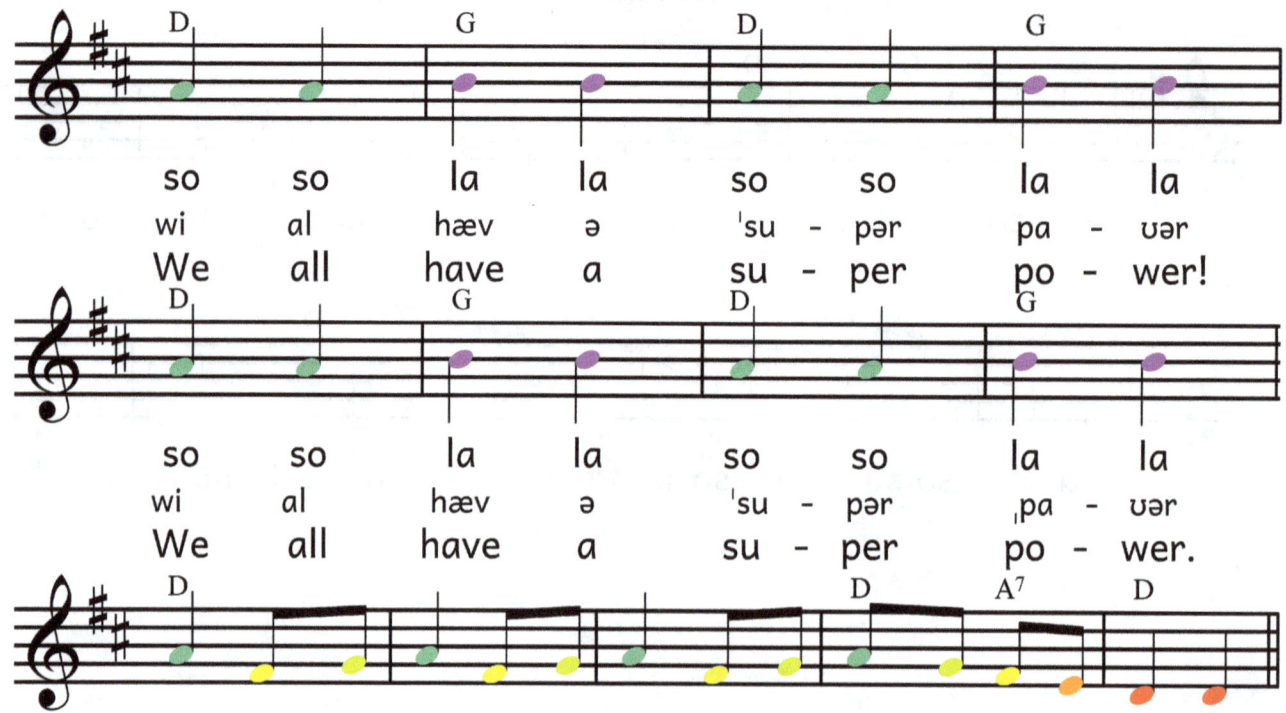

Español
Todos tenemos un superpoder
Music: Mexico (Chocolate molinillo)

69

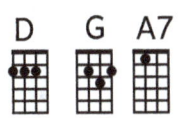

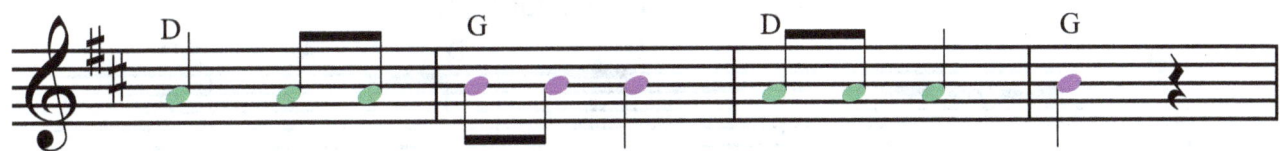

to - dos te - ne - mos un su - per - po - 'ðer
To - dos te - ne - mos un su - per - po - der

to - dos te - ne - mos un su - per - po - 'ðer
To - dos te - ne - mos un su - per - po - der!

a - 'pren - de de la is - 'tor - ja, kre - 'se i
A - pren - de de la hi - sto - ria, cre - se y

a - ju - 'ða a 'o - tros
a - yu - da a o - tros.

Traditional Song: Chocolate molinillo

tʃo ko 'la te mo li ni ʝo ko rɛ ko re, ke te pi ʝo
Chocolate molinillo, Corre corre, que te pillo

ko rɛ ras ko rɛ ras pɛ ro no me pi ʝa ras
Correrás, correrás, pero no me pillarás

Chocolate, whisk, run, run, or I'll catch you.
You will run, you will run, but you won't catch me.

Copyright © 2024 Sarah Samuelson Studio

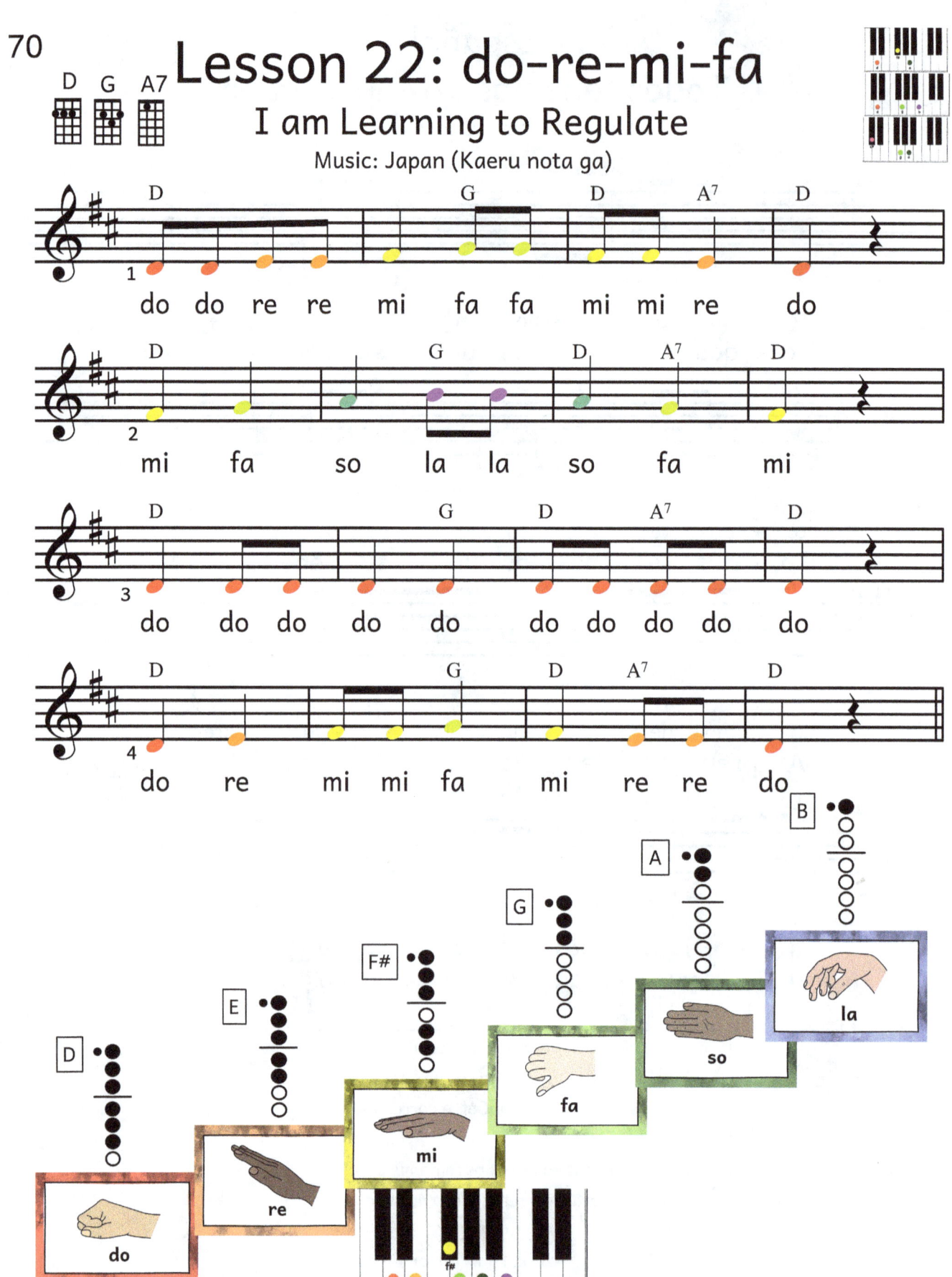

English
I am Learning to Regulate

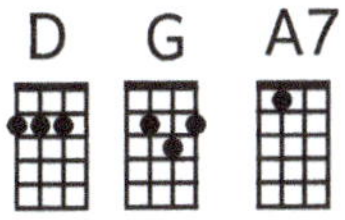

Music: Japan (Kaeru nota ga)

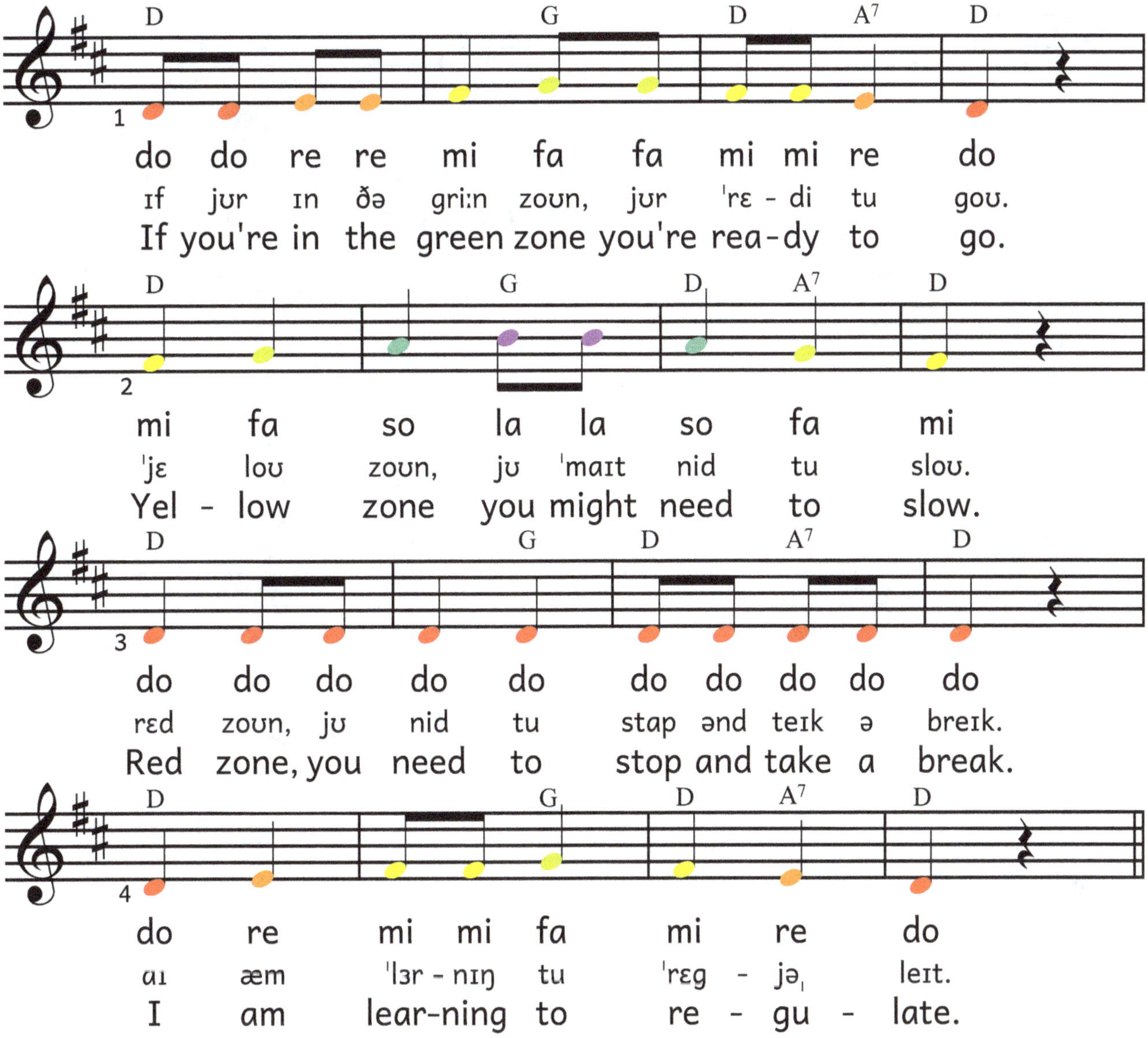

Japanese
Kaeru No Uta
Text & Music: Japan Folk Song

73

ka - ɛ - ru no u - ta ga
Ka e - ru no u - ta ga.

ki - ko ɛ - tɛ ku - ru jo
Ki - ko - e - te ku - ru yo

gwa   gwa   gwa   gwa
Gwa! Gwa! Gwa! Gwa!

gɛ - ro gɛ - ro gɛ - ro gɛ ro gwa gwa gwa
Ge - ro, Ge - ro, Ge - ro, Ge - ro Gwa! Gwa! Gwa!

Translation of Japanese:
The frog's song
we can hear it.
Gwa is like a frog sound.

Copyright © 2024 Sarah Samuelson Studio

Piano Chords & Intervals key of G

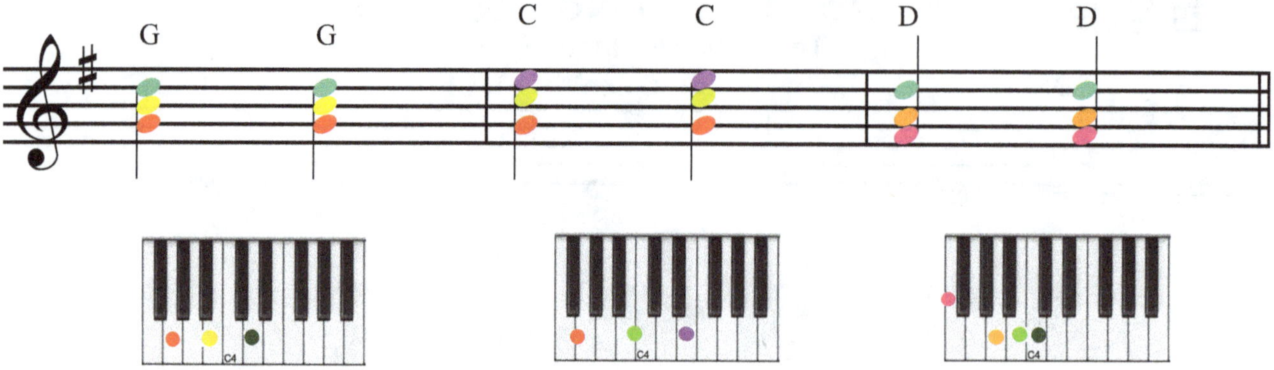

Seconds

do re mi fa so la so fa mi re do

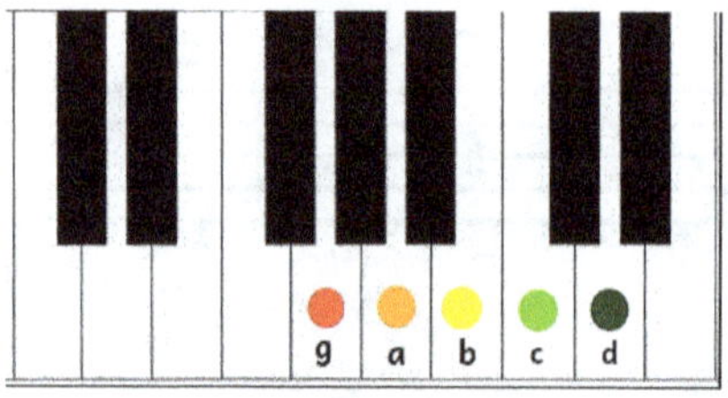

Thirds   Fourths   Fifths

do mi so mi fa re mi la so re so do do so

Guitar Chords key of G

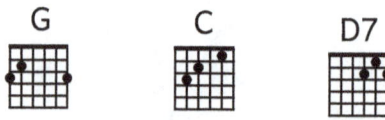

Guitar Chords key of D

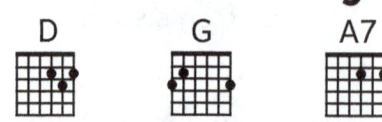

Copyright © 2023 Sarah Samuelson Studio

International Phonetic Alphabet Guides

IPA – English version

[a] October	[o] okay	[d] day	[l] last	[ʃ] shoe
[æ] ask	[ɔ] all	[f] few	[m] me	[j] yet
[e] vacation	[u] school	[ʒ] genre	[n] nest	[θ] three
[ɛ] bed	[ʊ] good	[g] go	[ŋ] sing	[t] today
[ə] taken	[ʌ] up	[h] how	[p] place	[ð] mother
[i] we	[b] be	[dʒ] just	[ɹ] right	[v] voice
[ɪ] if	[tʃ] child	[k] kite	[s] say	[w] when

IPA - Español version

[a] chocolate	[j] rey	[ã] elefante	[l] lino	[s] saco
[e] bebé	[w] cuatro	[ẽ] amen	[m] madre	[θ] cereal
[ɛ] bendito	[b] bestia	[f] fase	[n] nido	[t] tía
[ə] taken	[β] braβo	[g] gato	[ɲ] mañana	[x] ojo
[i] di, y	[tʃ] chocolate	[ɣ] siɣno	[p] pozo	[ʎ] caballo
[o] sol	[d] cuando	[ɟ] ayuno	[r] carro	
[u] su	[ð] dádiva	[k] kilo	[ɾ] braβo	

IPA - Brazilian Português

[a] aqui	[o] você	[ĩ] cinco	[ʒ] vejo	[r] cara
[ɐ] coisa	[ɔ] só	[õ] bom	[j] noite	[ɲ] tenho
[e] você	[u] tudo	[ũ] mundo	[w] quase	[dʒ] cidade
[ɛ] até	[ɐ̃] dança	[g] algo	[ʎ] filho	[tʃ] noite
[i] isso	[ẽ] tempo	[ʃ] baixo	[ʁ] ser	

IPA - Kreyòl-Ayisyen

[a] pale	[i] li	[u] ou	[œ̃] tan	[ʃ] chita
[e] beni	[ɔ] kom	[y] plume	[ɛ̃] incroyable	[tʃ] chicken
[ɛ] Senyè	[o] opere	[õ] kontan	[ʒ] Jesus	[j] yereswa
[ə] je				

Bibliography

Books

Adler, D. (1996). *The Kids' Catalog of Jewish Holidays.* Jewish Publication Society.

Bronstein, H. (1974). *A Passover Haggadah.* Central Conference of American Rabbis.

Burleigh, H.T. *Negro Spirituals arranged by H.T. Burleigh.* Art Song Central.

Campbell, P. (2014). *Music in Childhood from Preschool through the Elementary Grades.* Cengage Learning.

Carpenter, D. (2001). *African American Heritage Hymnal: 575 Hymns, Spirituals, and Gospel Songs.* GIA Publications.

Church of God in Christ Publishing Board. (1982). *Yes, Lord! Hymnal.* Church of God in Christ Publishing House.

Emmerson, J. (2014). *The Complete Illustrated Children's Bible.* Harvest House Publishers.

Hayes, R. (1948). *My Songs Panels 1, 2 & 3.* Little Brown and Company.

Giovanni, N. (2009). *On my journey now: Looking at African-American history through the spirituals.* Candlewick Press.

Glover, S. (1845) *History of the Norwich Sol-fa.* Norwich: Jarrold & Sons.

Musleah, R. (1999). *Why On This Night: A Passover Haggadah for Family Celebration.* Simon & Schuster.

Nicholls, K. (2020). *My Favourite Bible Stories For Children Around the World.* Harper Collins Publishers.

Orozco, J. (1994). *De Colores and Other Latin-American Folk Songs.* Puffin Books.

Various. (2002). *The Complete Jewish Songbook.* Transcontinental Music Publications.

White, C. (2006). *Tryin' to Get Ready: 30 African American Spirituals Arranged for SATB Voices.* GIA Publications.

Wilcox, C. (2003). *He Mele Aloha: A Hawaiian Songbook.* 'Oli'Oli Productions, L.L.C.

Zondervan. (2005). *The Beginner's Bible.* Zonderkidz.

Bibles

Aramaic Peshitta New Testament Translation. (2006). Light of the Word Ministry.

Bauscher, G. (2007) *HPBT Holy Peshitta Bible Translation.* Lulu Publishing.

Smith, J. (1876) *Smith Literal Translation.* Hartford American Publishing Co.

Websites:

www.bethsnotesplus.com

www.biblehub.com

www.mamalisa.com

www.easypronunciation.com

www.internationalphoneticassociation.org

www.ipanow.com

www.michaelkravchuk.com

www.stepbible.org

Special Thanks to Individuals

Katie African at Fivrr - Book Front & Back Covers

Daniele Leano - Português pronunciation

Priscilla Ozodo-Acevedo - voice coach and friend who has encouraged me so much in this project

Marie Polynice – Kreyòl Ayisyen (Haitian-Creole)

Christina Sanchez – Español pronunciation and sister and friend

Andriana Seay – voice coach and friend who has also encouraged me and helped me with singing

My wonderful husband, daughters, parents and sisters!

About Sarah Samuelson

Sarah Samuelson earned a Bachelor in Music Education from the University of Puget Sound, a Masters in Music Ed from Minnesota State Univ, and National Board Certification in Early Childhood Music Education. She has 15 years experience teaching music education in public schools and 6 years of teaching music education courses at the University of Puget Sound. She shared the ways that she adapted curriculum for the music classes for special education students she taught and for students with 504 plans. She has also used her skills in languages to meet needs of multilingual learners. In her private studio, Sarah has continued to learn from students with special needs, including students with Autism spectrum disorder, Trisomy 21 (Down syndrome), and students with language impairment. Combining these areas of knowledge and experience, Sarah created Learn to Sing in Harmony, a song-based method with an empathy theme to learn to read music for schools and homeschool learning. The curriculum is based on Kodaly method and incorporating folk songs from many different countries and African American spirituals from the United States and notes use the colors of the popular boomwhackers and recorders. Learn to Sing in Harmony Bible version for Christian-based learning and it follows the stories in multiple children's Bibles so that there is a song for every story. Since 2020 she has been participating in monthly Courageous Conversations (based on the Glenn Singleton book and curriculum) led by Dr. Connie Sims, reading books and watching movies and documentaries to increase her awareness and understanding of racial inequality. The books have four levels and progress in music theory with the goal being the joy of harmony! Sarah studied classical singing in her undergrad and grad programs and has performed in operas and musicals. She has been continuing her vocal growth learning new technique from vocal coaches, Onyedikachi Priscilla Ozodo-Acevedo and Andriana Seay, to sing outside of the classical genre and style especially in the areas of multiethnic & gospel worship and jazz.

More Learn to Sing & Play in Harmony Books

Learn to Sing Bible Versions

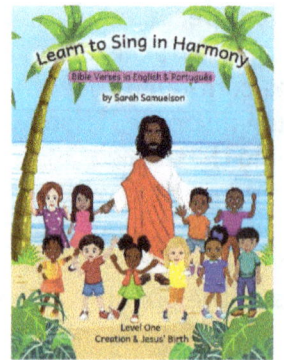 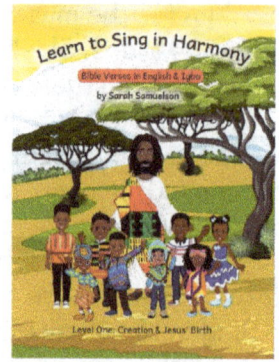 

Learn to Play Recorder Books   Empathy Books for Schools

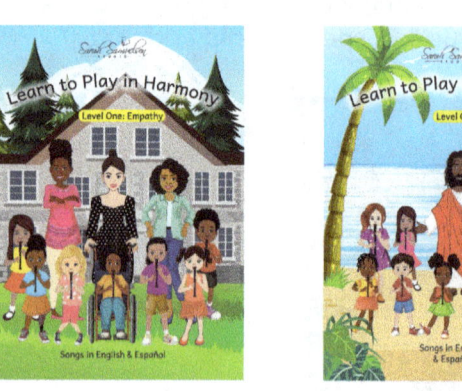 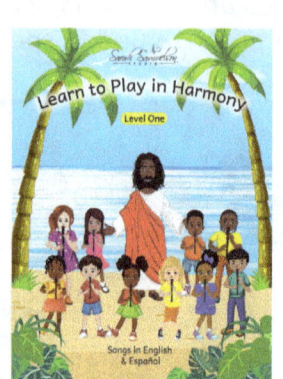  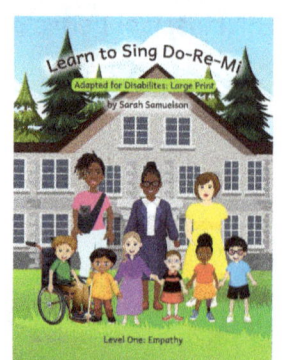

Jump-start Versions   Adapted for Disabilities

   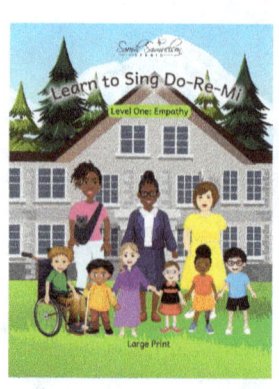

Date	Assignment	M	T	W	Th	F	S	S
Date	Assignment	M	T	W	Th	F	S	S

Date	Assignment	M	T	W	Th	F	S	S

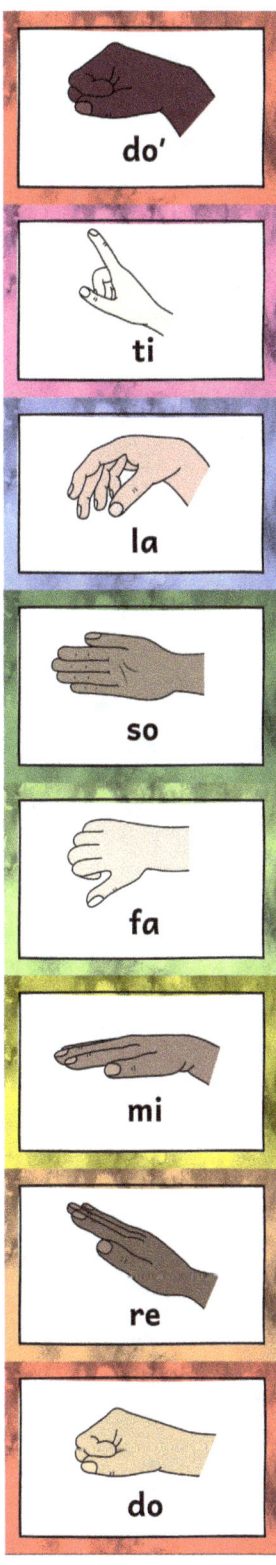

Copyright © 2024 Sarah Samuelson Studio
All Rights Reserved.

No part of this publication may be reproduced or transmitted in any form
without permission from the publisher.

www.ingramcontent.com/pod-product-compliance
Lightning Source LLC
Chambersburg PA
CBHW080415170426
43194CB00015B/2824